945.5
M425
1998

THE HILLS OF
TUSCANY

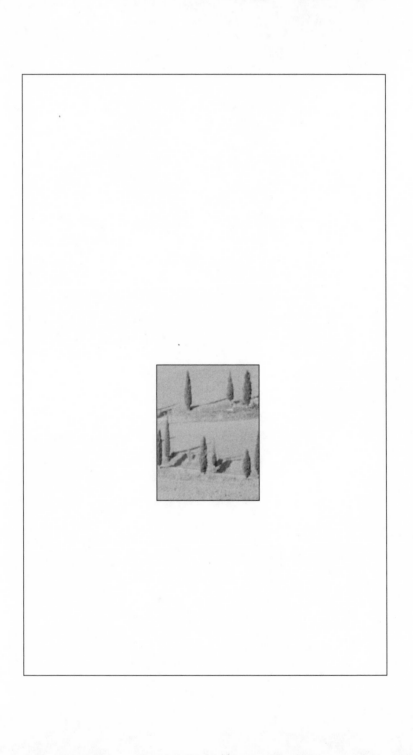

THE HILLS OF
TUSCANY

*A New Life
in an old Land*

FERENC MÁTÉ

ALBATROSS PUBLISHING HOUSE

The text of this book is composed in Adobe Garamond

Book design, illustrations and composition by Candace Máté
Manufactured by R.R. Donnelley

ISBN 0-920256-38-4
1 2 3 4 5 6 7 8 9 0

An *Albatross* book, distributed by:
W.W. NORTON . 500 FIFTH AVE . NEW YORK . NEW YORK 10110

For Candace
Forever

ACKNOWLEDGEMENTS

My gratitude to dearest Candace for all her help with the structuring of the book, and everlasting thanks to Starling Lawrence, W.W. Norton's editor-in-chief, for his masterful editing. And my profound thanks to all the people in the book, without whose generous friendship, I would have had nothing to write about.

CONTENTS

THE HILLS OF
TUSCANY

PART I

1 ~ THE LIGHT IN TUSCANY

September 1987 ~ Tuscany

We stepped from the cool shadows of the archway into the warmth of the autumn sun. It was early afternoon, the narrow, flagstone streets were deserted, the shops closed; Tuscany was eating. Arm in arm in the autumn light, calmed by the warmth and the pitcher of red wine we had with lunch, we ambled in contented silence up the hill toward the *piazza* where the mosaic facade of the cathedral blazed like a million tiny stars.

We had been shivering while researching a book in the rain of Sweden, the cold of Finland, and the damp of Brittany, and in more than a month this was the first time we were warm. We stared at the mosaics. Then, glitter-blinded and wine-weakened, we went around to the small church garden, sat on a low stone wall, and like dreamers through the centuries before us, gazed out over the countryside below.

A sea of hills rolled to the horizon, covered by odd-shaped, lovingly kept vineyards and olive groves, orchards and fields: a freshly plowed field here, a bit of corn there, some hay, some woods, some pasture, all odd sizes, all open and unfenced. The plots were defined by the curve of a stream, or the crook of a hill, or the fold of a hollow, with boundaries of poplars or a ditch or nothing. Old stone houses were huddled on knolls surrounded by their cypresses, fruit trees, and vegetable gardens. On a ridge, in a wood, a monastery stood with a square steeple, and beyond it a tiny hamlet on a hilltop. Everything was small—to the measure of man. And over it all reigned the gentle Tuscan light, and silence, and a calm.

Candace was far away, her gaze fixed near the horizon, auburn hair glowing in the sinking sun. The air thickened with light. We sat.

After a while I suggested moving on.

Candace gazed. "You know," she finally said, "I'm getting tired of moving on. We've been 'moving on' for fifteen years. The houseboat, the sailboat, the mountain cabin, that garage in Laguna Beach, the attic in Paris, the cubbyhole in New York, the whatsit in the Bahamas. What was that thing with eight sides anyway?"

A tolling of bells from the monastery trembled in the air, sonorous and slow, drifting like a veil of melancholy over the silent hills.

"They're burying someone," Candace softly said, and looked as if it were someone she had known. When the bells were still and their echo had died away, the world remained respectfully silent. The sun sank behind strips of clouds and the air glittered with light. After a while, just below the town, rose the brittle sound of kindling being cut. Then a woman's voice, one accustomed to shouting, *"Mario! Non troppo grosso! Per la Madonna!"*

I laughed. "What did she say?" I asked Candace.

"She said she was sick and tired of moving on, and if she had to move on one more time, she was moving on on her own and leaving you behind like camel dung in the desert."

Mario chopped for a while, unhurriedly, rhythmically. The kindling must have been *"non troppo grosso,"* for no one gave him hell. Mario was toeing the line.

"I want to settle down," Candace said. "A tiny house, some fruit trees, a vegetable garden."

"Sounds nice," I said. "Where?"

"Anywhere." She had said that louder and it echoed from the church walls. An old man with a narrow brimmed hat who had wandered into the churchyard turned and looked at us as if he had been following the conversation. I looked out at the hills, the warmth, the gentleness. "How about here?" I said, spreading a hand toward the valley below.

"Here?"

"Lots of room for vegetables. We could get an old farmhouse and fix it up. Have a bit of land, some woods, a few rows of grapes, a wine cellar. Make our own wine. Old wood casks oozing that perfume, pigeons swooping overhead. A rooster on the dunghill. Olives. Can you imagine pressing our own olive oil, pouring it on a hunk of fire-toasted bread with a ton of garlic rubbed over it?"

"You're nuts," she laughed.

"Fine, a bit of garlic."

"I mean about settling here."

"Why not? The country is beautiful; the food the best; the people are wonderful, art even better. Concerts in churches and castles. I'll write, you paint. Even the weather is perfect. What more is there? We could have a little farm right there." And I pointed just over Mario's head at a small farmhouse near whose crumbling walls a handful of white somethings were grazing in the shade.

"A farm. You don't know a thing about a farm."

"I can learn."

"But you don't speak a word of Italian!"

"I'll take a course."

She smiled. "You don't even know where you are."

"I'll ask somebody."

She stared at me in silence. So did the old man, his face aglow with anticipation. Candace's eyes softened. "You're a nice guy," she said, like an attendant calming a mental patient. "But you and reality just don't mix," and she shook her head. The old man seemed satisfied with that. He adjusted his hat and left. The pulleys of the bells in the tower above us rumbled, the pins creaked, and with a great "whoosh" the enormous old bell swung out of the tower, then a wider swing, swoooshhh, then a deafening "Diiiinggg" then another "Donnggg," booming and thundering until both the air and earth shook. A short priest with large hands shuffled into the church, followed by some older women in ones and twos.

Candace got up. She seemed deep in thought. "You know," she said, "there are few things more scary than moving to a foreign country."

"Name one," I said.

2 ~ TURN LEFT
AT THE MADONNA

*F*or the next year we lived walled-in in New York City, Candace working long hours to complete her Master's in Fine Arts, while I finished a book about sailboats, then struggled with a novel about some poor sailor searching for his dead wife. The degree was completed and the novel, too. The latter was placed with care in the bottom of a wooden chest where—I hoped—it could somehow improve with age like wine, and emerge a few years hence, supple and complex.

Anyway, the year passed.

Most mentally stable people, given this gift of time, would have sobered up from daydreams of living in Tuscany, gotten a job, and signed up with a gym and cable channels. But not I. I planned. Determined to find a place to rent for a month from which I could hunt for the Tuscan Farmhouse of My Dreams, I made calls: the Italian tourist board, Italian travel agents, an American university in Tuscany, an order of Benedictine monks near Florence, the corner pizza-parlor whose owner was Korean but had postcards from Sienna taped to the register, and even the local Italian Golden Age

Club, where everyone turned out to be deaf. Nothing worked. No one knew a thing. Or if they did, they weren't talking. Or when they did, it was in Italian and I didn't understand a word. Then I found a contact through a chance encounter: in the laundry room.

Planning in advance was new to me. I usually wing it, not because I'm adventurous, just lazy. Sometimes it works. Fifteen years earlier, Candace and I, vagabonding around Central America in our Volkswagen camper on seven dollars a day, got to "discover" the Mayan ruins of Tikal, fabled to every one but us. There we were, deep in the Guatemalan jungle, fishtailing in a thunderstorm axle-deep in mud, escaping a canvas-covered truck full of either murderous hit-squad killers or melons. When I'm lost in the jungle in the middle of a revolution, stopping to clarify the contents of suspicious trucks is not a priority.

At long last the truck faded in the downpour, stuck sideways on a hill—God bless you, Mr. Volkswagen, whoever you are—when Candace says to me, "What are those great bumps in the jungle up ahead?" I immediately thought "Enemy!" but the bumps were enormous and immobile, jungle-covered things, pointy—like when you stick your toes up under a bedsheet—except there were dozens of them the size of tall, steep pyramids, which, to our speechless surprise, they in fact turned out to be.

Winging it in a camper is one thing: you can just bump along until you find a place you like. But you can't just land in Tuscany and yell out, "Anybody here have a place to rent?" So I planned. And it worked.

~

The autumn sun sat low in the sky as we wound through the Tuscan hills. The Matra, a little sports car we had bought when we

"As I was saying," I said, "perfect paradise."

~

We were giddy. We ran around the house like fools, then grabbed the emergency bottle of French wine from the car, warm but who cared, and the emergency brie and bread we kept for such occasions, and straddled the stone wall on the terrace, just as the sun dipped and the sky caught fire and enormous shafts of light shot across the sky. We drank, passing the bottle, then the world around us started gushing colors. The olives glowed silver, geraniums blushed, the ancient walls and worn brick walks oozed centuries of hues. And the air was drenched with the fragrance of forest and sage, lavender, rosemary, autumn earth and sun-warmed stone. We ate, and slugged back the wine, and got drunk, and hugged, and it got dark. "The *trattoria* is closing soon," I said. "We'd better go and eat."

"And drink," Candace said.

God bless the Irish.

~

We showered, dried our hair by the fire and went out into the autumn night. A great dome of stars shimmered over us. The dark forest was alive: things rustled, frogs croaked, and something made sharp little yelps as it moved through the hedge. We wound back through the blackened woods, the headlights throwing looming shadows everywhere, through the tiny hamlet with a warm glow in its windows, and past the last house where a fire burned and the smell of chicken coops mingled with the smoke, and an old man rammed a pitchfork in the coals and made sparks fly toward the stars.

About a mile down the road in an isolated house stood the Trattoria del Cacciatore. Lights were on inside and smoke wafted from the chimney into the fields. We went in under a *pergola*. An old lady was sewing behind a tiny bar; around her were stacks of spices, soaps and vegetables. She greeted us with a quiet *"buona sera"* and waved us into the bigger room ahead. It was a clean, whitewashed place, with wood beams and terra-cotta floors, its few tables set with impeccable white linen, and behind an archway in a waist-high fireplace, a hot-coaled wood-fire glowed. There was a little girl of about three carrying a doll and calling, *"Mamma, Mamma, c'è gente."* This was indeed worthy news, for although it was well past eight, we were and seemingly had been the only *gente* there. Then Mamma came, a shy woman of about thirty, and said something and pointed at the table near the fire. We sat. On the table stood an unlabeled bottle of red wine. The fire glowed. The little girl put the doll on the chair between us and started talking to it gently, looking at each of us in turn, and then at it again, informing and instructing, and even waving a finger telling it to behave. Candace talked to her and she replied with a most serious face, then she whispered to her doll and went away. I pulled the cork and poured us wine. Candace raised her glass. "Welcome home," she said.

The food was as simple as the place. For appetizers there were assorted *crostini*—fire-toasted bread, some smeared with chicken liver, others with sautéed mushrooms. Then of course came pasta. We both had *pici*—a homemade, hand-rolled, unevenly thick spaghetti—Candace with a sauce of wild boar and I with a sauce of mixed wild mushrooms. We were slow in eating, savoring every bite, and looked up as the little girl's Mamma came and asked if the sauces were fine. Candace complimented her on the food and apologized for eating so slowly. A big smile broke on her face, *"Piano, piano, con calma,"* she said. Slowly, slowly, with calm. Then came the meats: for Candace roasted pheasant with parchment-like brown skin, and for me wild boar stew marinated in red wine and juniper berries and tasting like heaven, and a plate of Tuscan white beans drenched in olive oil and crushed garlic, and a salad. And we kept emptying wine glasses, toasting the little girl, her Mamma, Tuscany, the boar, the beans, the toasts.

We ate, with *calma*, and drank, with gusto, and the little girl and her doll had said good night long ago, led upstairs by *Nonna*, Grandma, from behind the bar, and then Mamma went up, too, to say good night, and we swooned from the heat of the fire and the wine, and thank God Nonna came back and brought us two espressos to bring us to, then she quickly thought it over and brought two glasses of *grappa*, to sink us once again.

As we left, they both came and said good-bye—handshakes and smiles as if we had been acquaintances for years. Then we went out into a silver flood of moonlight.

We breathed the night air deeply, utterly content. And it wasn't just the food and wine, but also that family. There was something heartening in seeing three generations together there— at home. We felt as if we had had dinner at someone's house. And the place was so honest, unpretentious, that you knew what counted was not the walls and floors, but the people they comforted. And it felt reassuring that the vegetables came from their gardens, the wine from the small vineyard across the road, and that the boar and the pheasant were hunted by Grandpa. We talked about this as we ambled in the moonlight, until Candace said, "Did we drink all that wine just to discuss social science?" We hurried home.

The bedding was cool and white, and through the window blazed the moon and threw shadows of wind-swayed branches on the walls.

3 ~ THREE HUNDRED MILLION!?

*T*he next morning we leapt from the bed to open the shutters and see the world around us. The windowsill was already warm from the sun. Tatters of white fog nestled in the valleys and hill towns glowed in the distance in early light. The leaves of the great oaks quivered in the wind, and somewhere in the woods the Angel of the Key was yelling at her wards, "Yee, yee." Birds were everywhere. Finches pecked at the seeds in fallen pinecones, jays riddled ripe apples, and over the crest of the hill where a tractor could be heard, a falcon circled, awaiting the mice to be plowed from their burrows. Something moved in the forest beside the house. A moment later an old man, almost as gaunt as the Angel of the Key, stuck his head into the sunlight, met our eyes, and his bony face burst into a schoolboy smile. He pulled himself free from the scrub, yanked a wicker basket after him, held it up toward us and, still smiling, yelled, *"Funghi!"*

Candace's face paled. Even her freckles. And she said almost hoarsely, *"Porcini."* And she was gone. She hopped across the room pulling on her jeans, threw a leather jacket over her naked shoulders and thundered down the stairs and out into the sun. They chatted back and forth hovering over the *funghi* like witches at a cauldron, pulling things out, admiring. Then she turned and held toward me two great bulbous things with dark velvety skin that were replicas of mushrooms I had seen in books of fairytales. "Tonight we really eat," she said beaming. The old man said a string of incomprehensible words, to which I replied—exhausting much of my Italian vocabulary— *"Stupendo. Grazie."* Then he turned, fought his way back into the woods and vanished.

"Smell these! Smell these!" came the voice from down below. I went. Candace was in the kitchen holding up a mushroom as if it were the Holy Grail. The kitchen was full of a pungent, sweet-dank odor. "We're grilling these tonight," she said victoriously.

We had breakfast on the terrace in the sun. The invisible owners of the villa had left emergency rations of sugar and coffee, so we made some cappuccinos and ate the remnants of our baguette and brie with some apples we picked from the tree below. The sun was climbing high. It was time for adventure. Candace had to paint two more paintings for a show, but I was free. Free to go to find us a house in Tuscany.

Before I left, I gave her a hand setting up in the spare room on the garden. We moved furniture, fabricated an easel from boards and stretched two canvases on frames she'd brought dismantled from New York, then she said, "It's stuffy in here," and went to open the French doors and their shutters.

Hell fell. Within a blink of an eye, the quiet garden room metamorphosed into a scene from the movie that Alfred Hitchcock should have made but didn't: *The Bugs*. That hand-wide space between the glass and shutters was refuge for all the crawly creepy floppy insects of the world, and now, with their haven wrecked, they swarmed and zoomed, buzzed and droned, crept and leapt all over the tranquillity of our poor, bloody lives. The air was full of them; the floor alive with them; wasps, flies, ants, centipedes, stink-bugs and red-bugs, moths and flying things darkened earth and sky.

We counter-attacked. I with a broom, Candace with a feather duster. We swiped and trashed and pushed them toward the door, but many turned and came again.

We stood there pouring sweat, ankle deep in slaughter. The exterminators. Candace went out onto a sunlit patch of grass and spat. Shook a few cadavers from her hair than spat again. Shook out her shirt and watched a few more fall. Then she said dearly, "Exactly as you promised, Darling. Bloody paradise."

~

I drove to town. The vineyards were aglow but silent. In the olive groves men walked carrying wooden ladders and folded nets, getting ready to pick olives. A black cloud drifted overhead, but past its edge, streams of sunshine poured into the fields. I parked outside the medieval walls and walked in on the lumpy stones through the soaring arch of the town gate and its giant, iron-spiked doors whose wood was ancient and cracked and gray. A clap of thunder rumbled through the streets and it began to rain; I hoisted my umbrella. The rain swept down and slicked the stones, and the shopkeepers ran from the perches outside their doors where they had been standing, leaning, gossiping with each other, with passersby, ran and stood dejected behind their glasspanes streaked with rain, ruing their rain-imposed exile to silence.

Few of the shops had signs; you could see what they sold through the windows so why bother; besides, everyone in the tiny town knew exactly where to go. So I walked carefully, evaluating the contents of every window, for I had been told by our Californian go-between to look for one with a few ragged antiques, with *Assicurazione*, Insurance, written on the door, where inside Signor Neri actually sells houses. And pigs and cows when his neighbors ask him. And makes arrangements, when needed, for local funerals.

I found it. I stood in the rain and gazed at a shop window with an old oil painting stuck between a mirror and a milking stool. It was a painting of a sad saint studying a skull. Inside the vaulted space Signor Neri was behind a much-used table, buried in cigarette smoke, talking on the phone, waving about an arm as if conducting his life. I froze. I couldn't muster the courage to go in. I tilted the umbrella to hide my face and moved on in the rain. I had no trouble at all with four of Neri's professions, but the fifth one definitely conjured up some shivers. I realize that a man of forty should have developed a sense of life's stages, accepting the fact that his youth is now behind him, that all things lead at some point to an end. But to go in there and face the man who will be, so to speak, nailing shut my coffin, well I'm sorry, but I needed a bit more time. I needed a bit more time to confront the inevitable, that one day fairly soon, perhaps not tomorrow but nearer with every day, comes that destined moment when that limitless thing so full of daily wonder ends, and you have to, with irrevocable finality, buy a house and settle down.

The rain stopped. The shopkeepers dove back onto the street already talking before their feet touched the stones. People eased themselves out of the doorways of their houses and cafes. I closed my umbrella. I had reached the outer fortifications of town—the wall loomed before me. There was nowhere else to go. I turned back. Besides, I had sort of prepared. I had prepared for the inevitable by learning all the words and phrases I deemed a must for the occasion: *rudere*, ruin, *casa colonica*, old country house, *muri*, walls, *tetto*, roof, *trave*, beams, *pavimento*, floors, *inedificabile*, unbuildable, along with a few life-and-death words like *sì*, *no*, and of course *quanto costa*. So I poised my rolled umbrella and walked steadfastly back, mumbling *trave*, *muri*, *rudere*, and *casa* under my breath.

The street was now full of people, mostly women, with a scattering of old male pensioners. The women were loaded down with bags from the morning's shopping: fresh bread from the baker, meats from the butcher, fruit and vegetables from the greengrocer, while the men huffed and puffed lugging the morning paper. The windows began to open overhead and out poured the smell of simmering sauces and fresh baking, and out came a few heads to join the gossip down below. I walked with firm decision.

I was modestly pleased with how well my Italian was going. I said *"Buongiorno, che bella giornata,"* to a complete stranger. Surely I was ready for Signor Neri. I knew words and phrases, hell, whole paragraphs. I'll show him from the start that he's not dealing with no fool. *Buongiorno. Che bella giornata. Mi chiamo* Ferenc Máté, *sono uno scrittore da* New York, *cerco una bella casa colonica,* and so on.

I had completely erased from my mind the humiliation of last summer. When crossing into Germany, Candace suggested we learn some basic phrases. I went red with indignation. *Me*, learn German?! Hadn't I escaped from Hungary to Austria? Gone to school there? Spoke German like a German? Candace gently mentioned that since then thirty years had passed, but I was too insulted to listen. So I charged into the little Bavarian inn, planted my feet confidently before a charming Frau, smiled and began effortlessly my usual amicable discourse with a hearty *"Guten abend."* Normally my chitchat would include compliments about the countryside, the town, and local food and wine. So, I casually and confidently began, *"Guten abend,"* and then, without warning, I went completely deaf. I must have. I couldn't hear a thing. I couldn't hear a single word about schnapps or liebfraumilch, or the Bavarian Alps, not a word of all the poetic phrases I must have been uttering. Just silence.

But that was a different year, a different country. This time I *had* practiced. I had it all down pat, every word, every phrase, every nuance, even intonation, even a bit of Italian waving of the arms. I was prepared.

I swung open the shop door, marched up to Signor Neri who had now finished his telephone discussion, smiled reassuringly to put him at his ease, and began. *"Buongiorno. Mi chiamo* Ferenc Máté. *Sono uno scrittore da* New York, *stiamo cercando una casa colonica,"* and on and on. It positively flowed. My mouth and brain were now on automatic, the tone melodious, even the arms waving. Flawless. Signor Neri listened with what seemed to me approval, nodded, inserted, *"Ho capito"* now and then, and when I reached deep for long words like *"preferibilmente,"* even seemed touched by admiration. Then I finished. I had done it. I had conquered Italian. Tuscany lay at my feet. Signor Neri stood up. I'm not sure what I had in fact expected, perhaps a quick applause, congratulatory handshake, even a quick tour of his favorite coffins, but instead he did a most devastating thing: he replied.

In long sentences.

That went on forever.

I felt faint. I stood there mouth agape trying to grab a familiar word from the hurricane of noise around me. But Neri was merciless. He talked on. And then an added horror came over me that maybe he *hadn't* understood me at all, and maybe he was at this very moment discoursing *not* about old houses, but about insurance, or a chair, or a milk cow, or a coffin.

Then in that desperate moment the sun came to my rescue. It had burst into the street, and from the old mirror that leaned against the saint, a beam of sunlight lit a photo of an old Tuscan farmhouse pinned on the wall beside me. It had a fine outbuilding and outside stairs, half-covered by brambles. *"In vendita?"* I blurted hoarsely. For sale?

Neri halted his interminable oration, looked at the photo, looked at me, seemingly gauging if I was worthy of the place, then responded solemnly, *"Forse."* Maybe.

I was shocked. "Maybe?" Whoever heard of such unprofessional conduct? We don't talk like that in America, dammit. We call an agent, set a price, sign a listing. Done. Black and white. Clear as day. But not in Tuscany. Here, as I was to find out before nightfall, things work not by any rigid laws or rules, but by instantly evaporating undercurrents of rumor. The First Commandment in Tuscany seems to be, "Thou shalt never put anything in writing—for then how the hell can you possibly change your mind?" This of course is not found *written* in the Bible for obvious reasons. It manifests itself most noticeably in For Sale signs. There aren't any. Nor is anything ever communicated directly to a real estate agent—who of course doesn't exist on paper—by the seller, who doesn't exist with much certainty either, but rather through some mutually barely known, and reciprocally wouldn't-trust-the-bastard-as-far-as-I-could-throw-him third party. And Signor Neri demonstrated in the next hour exactly how this worked. He motioned for us to go, and we went out, with him shutting the door quickly lest the cigarette smoke escape and spoil the ambiance.

The sun beat down and the cobblestones steamed, and people moved at ease through the autumn air. The doors and windows were now open wide, and fragrances of roasting meats and rosemary tumbled into the street. Tuscany was gearing up for *pranzo*. This daily meal of at least four courses, resembling in quantity our average Thanksgiving dinner, usually begins at one and ends when the last person falls unconscious. But it was now just after eleven and the sauces were barely half done simmering, the meats half done roasting, so the street was full of people grouped in twos and threes and fours chatting or walking, old with old, old with young, anyone with anyone, cats with dogs, all discussing only God knows what.

The beauty of not understanding a thing people say around you is that—if you are an optimist like me—you'll always romanticize and think the very best. You will think that the melodious voice of the old lady selling eggs off a two-wheeled cart under the arches is recalling some profound moment from her youth, when in fact you find out later she was cursing the chicken-shit that stuck stubbornly to the shells. And similarly you might think a young mother is murmuring words of love and wisdom to her *tesoro* in the stroller, when in fact she's saying, "Shut up or I'll squash you, you insignificant error of bad timing." With a smile.

We turned abruptly from all this into a lane so narrow I could touch the buildings on either side, then up a few steps and into a tiny pizzeria, with a few linen-covered tables and a giant old brick oven that was now belching Sahara-grade heat waves over us, but mostly over the short, thin-haired, skin-and-bone *pizzaiolo*, who was poking at the hell-fire that raged before him. He was dressed in what must be the height of *pizzaiolo* fashion: pants, no socks, and patent leather shoes. Period. Neri and he went at it. The *pizzaiolo* was not overwhelmed by whatever it was Neri told him, objecting at first with one sweaty arm then the other, and at last he stretched both his arms toward the flames and pleaded, *"Porca Madonna. Che fo' con il fuoco? Dio cieco."*

I have found memorable phrases like these the best of foreign language lessons. First, at such emotional moments their enunciation is crystal clear. Second, the image of place, people and situation emblazoned on my mind, I can later recall details, for example, how the feminine noun *Madonna* has the adjective *porca,* meaning "pig," agree with it, hence the "a" ending, whereas the masculine *Dio*—God—takes its adjective with an "o," hence *cieco,* which means "blind." The more mundane part means, "What do I do with the fire?"

Neri touched my arm, flashed a victorious smile and said *"Un attimo."* Then the *pizzaiolo* made a phone call, donned a shirt and yelled, "Elena!" The most dazzling apparition of a black-haired Tuscan beauty in her twenties came in. The *pizzaiolo* gave instructions to Elena, and I was ushered out into the street where I was blinded by sunlight reflecting from the *pizzaiolo's* sockless ankles.

Signor Neri must have done good business with either his beasts or his humans—live or dead—for he put us into a Lancia and we zoomed past the tiny Fiat Cinquecentos and three-wheeler Apes. We roared up into the hills, and pulled up beside a tidy wood. We walked through woods, then a verdant pasture, and within a minute stood at the house. My knees began to shake. The ancient stone walls were two feet thick, with arched doorways and a terra-cotta roof of a hundred hues. An L-shaped outbuilding formed a yard, and in it stood a crumbling well. What else could you ask of life? The fact that it had no doors or windows, that some of the walls had crumbled, that the sun shone through the roof, was not enough to bring me back to reality. And Candace, the voice of reason, was far away. I went in and looked around.

I was shocked. There was nowhere to live. All the ground floor had been stables. The windows were few, small and very high, the walls lined with feeders, and the chipped and worn paving bricks were all built to channel rivers of urine. And while the last drop of urine had not flown there for years, its odor, having penetrated deep into brick and mortar, wafted in the warm and humid air. The Tuscan dream house turned out be a pigsty.

I turned to Signor Neri, but he was nowhere. I went back out and walked around the house, but there was no one; the empty hayfields ran to a woods below. A fine damned how do you do, leaving a prospective client in the wilderness? Why wasn't he here, giving me the sales pitch, pointing out features, amenities, the cross-hall dining room, the master bedroom ensuite? I had heard of some agents playing it cool, but this was overkill. Where the hell was his ambition? Didn't he want a bigger Lancia? Or another one? Or an electric golf-cart? With a chauffeur? Or a condo in Kenya? Didn't he bloody well want to get ahead?

In anger, I started hacking at the brambles with a stick, and there in their depth I sighted remnants of the long outside stairs I had seen in the photo. I bushwhacked my way up—brambles, prickles, nicks, cuts, squishy things below my feet. But at least there were signs of human habitation. At the top of the stairs, a massive double door swung open on giant pins. Bats flew. I was in a nasty little kitchen. It had a collapsed fireplace and a gaping hole in the roof where rain had poured in for years, melting plaster, rotting beams, turning the mortar between the paving bricks to mush. But most depressing were the doors. Four of them. The kitchen was a hallway. It led to three small, dull rooms and a tiny-windowed, suspended outhouse, where you could perform the barest of bare essentials and no more.

While standing there swamped by disillusion, I heard voices rising in the distance. It was Sockless and Neri. They were coming from the woods, side by side through the hayfield, arms waving, their voices rising and falling. I thought they were checking property lines or future road-access or something similar, but upon seeing me their faces lit up, and they both held up paper bags victoriously and yelled almost in chorus, *"Funghi!"*

Only much later did I learn that to understand what *funghi* means to a Tuscan, you have to look in America for emotionally loaded words like "Mom," except that Mom can't be picked in the woods in early autumn and eaten grilled with a bit of salt and oil. And this *funghi* hunting—especially for *porcini*, which at Balducci's on Sixth Avenue will cost you a day's pay *each*—is not only limited to wayward country folk, but is indeed a national pastime. It is common to see Mercedes Benzes and Masserattis of the most elegant Romans pulled over into the mud of autumn, men in jackets and women in fur coats and high heels, sunk to their knees in ditches, peering under bushes and leaves for the glow of the velvet caps. The calmest and most rational of doctors and professors will think nothing of rising at ungodly predawn hours, to rush to some secret site, whispered by informants, before others arrive and pick the spot bare. Anyway, Sockless and Neri kept coming. They were almost at the house when, so near to us that I almost died of fright, a cannon detonated and shook the air, and sent the bat and pigeon cloud into a frenzy overhead. A gentle, round-faced man came smiling from behind a bush, walked a ways into the field, reached down and rose with a pheasant in his hand.

"Porco Dio, Duillio. *Che bel fagiano,"* Sockless yelled toward him, and, not to be outdone, raised his sack of mushrooms and blared *"Funghi."* The three of them huddled for a while comparing just-found treasures, and then, without my knowing it, the sale of the house began in earnest.

Neri edged over to me, took my arm, whispered *"Padrone,"* which I gathered to mean owner, and ushered me a respectful distance from the other pair. After what seemed an eternity, Sockless turned and came toward us, lifting his alabaster ankles, like a trotter, over the hay. Then he and Neri huddled. This resulted in Neri's next one-word sentence to me—he was no fool, he had learned his lesson in the vault— *"Forse."* Maybe.

For the next while, Sockless flitted back and forth between Signor Funghi and Signor Fagiani, and there was huddling and arm waving at either end. No sooner would Sockless leave than Neri would literally dive under the nearest bush and poke and scratch for more *funghi.* When the negotiations reached a fever pitch, Neri got excited, ran to the trunk of a dead old olive around whose base grew a variable crown of pale brown mushrooms and roared, *"Duillio! Sei cieco? So' famiglioli!"* Whether this was a ploy or not, it worked—Duillio was rattled. He could not handle the continued loss of mushrooms and the sale of his hovel all at the same time.

Then Sockless returned, planted his feet and said, "Veri chip. *Tre cento milioni."*

I gasped for air. I tried to shift all the bloody zeros but could not be sure whether he wanted three thousand or three million dollars.

But Neri knew. He ran at Duillio and I thought for a moment he'd knock him down. He cursed him at the top of his voice, coupling the Madonna with a broad selection of wild and domestic beasts, turned violently away, and rushed off to another olive trunk, where he gathered up an armful of *famiglioli*. Then softly enough for the whole world to hear, he spoke a single word, *"Stronzo,"* which, I was told that night, is the tiny turd that concludes a very taxing movement.

That, I assumed, had been our counteroffer.

From the valley below rose the sound of church bells. It was one o'clock. Neri gave a wistful sigh, the anger of a second ago gone without a trace, and he took both me and Sockless by the arm and said, *"Ragazzi, mangiamo."* Kids, let's eat. And they turned back and yelled *"Buon appetito"* to Duillio, who stood forsaken with his shotgun and his pheasant. Then Duillio yelled out *"Aspettate,"* hauled his rotund body up the hill, and handed the bird to Neri. *"Un po' d'arrosto."* A little roast.

This, I assumed, was the counter to our counter.

On our way back to town, not a word was spoken about the house or Duillio. From what I could understand, the entire conversation was given to cooking *funghi* and the pheasant in a hundred different ways. We stopped in town. The streets were deserted. The clang of utensils and voices drifted from the windows. Tuscany was stuffing itself. Neri invited me for *pranzo*. Then Sockless invited both of us to his restaurant for *pranzo*. They argued. I cut in and tried explaining in Italian, French, some English, and some violent Hungarian curses when nothing else worked, that my wife was expecting me and she has red hair and when you're late she throws things at the door.

That they understood.

Then Neri said something that I took to mean, "Don't worry we can see lots of houses tomorrow," and handed me a card with his name and number, carefully avoiding all professions, and— *"Arrivederci, arrivederci"*—we parted.

4 ~ A HAMLET

The sparkling autumn light shimmered in halos around the cypresses. Nothing moved along the road or in the fields. As I passed through the hamlet, a cow tethered in the small sideyard of the chapel raised its head and shook its bell. Wood smoke wafted over the lichened clay tiles of the roofs. The woods were silent. The Matra ghosted down the dirt road to the house. The windows of the house were open wide, the plain cotton curtains fluttered in the breeze, and out floated Candace's voice, singing. She was singing "If I ever lose my head, da da da da dum." I went and sat in an old iron garden chair, closed my eyes, and let the sun warm me. Aromas of cooking drifted in the air, like meat roasting but wilder, more savory. When she changed from singing to humming, I called out, "Candace! Look out here, would you? Am I dead? Did I die and go to heaven without noticing?"

She leaned out the window, her red hair disheveled, her face flushed from the heat of the fire, beaming. "You ain't *begun* to die yet, Chum. Wait 'til you taste this."

The table was set with a checked tablecloth, some plain old

white china, and from somewhere she had gotten a fresh loaf of flat Tuscan bread, tomatoes that she had quartered onto a plate, a bottle of wine, a bottle of obscenely green and completely opaque olive oil, and some pasta which she now let slide into the boiling water.

"Where did you get all this?" I asked, amazed.

"The store, darling. The hamlet at the turn-off has a store."

"That's more than two miles. You walked?"

"My pal the *porcini* hunter gave me a ride there and back in his three-wheeler. I hope you're not jealous, but I think I have a beau."

I wasn't jealous. The guy was eighty-five if he was a day. Besides, I was used to Candace's hitchhiking. That was how we met. It was a sunny May Sunday in Vancouver, with fruit trees in blossom everywhere. I was in an ancient, beat-up, patched-up Porsche convertible, the round kind, that I had picked up for eight hundred dollars, the top was down, the sun pouring in. Candace was on an old three-speed bike, all flushed from riding, resting before tackling a long hill. Thank God there was a stop sign so I didn't need to invent an excuse to stop. She looked. I gawked. She smiled. I stopped breathing. She finally saved my life. "You want to give me a ride up the hill?" she asked.

"Sure," I said with my last bit of air. Then we piled the bike in the Porsche behind the seats and I couldn't sleep for days.

The year before that she had been even more audacious. When her semester ended at the University of Hawaii, she went down to the yacht harbor where all the sailboats from the Trans-Pac Race were resting, walked up to a crew folding up a sail on the foredeck of a cutter, smiled and said, "Could I get a ride to San Francisco?"

And she did. For twenty-seven days.

"*Tagliatelle con porcini,*" she announced.

When I started this memoir I swore I would not clutter it with dissertations about food, but I soon realized that writing about Tuscany without talking about food is like writing about the Titanic without mentioning that it sunk. We forked our *porcini* in reverential silence, and sipped our red wine. The *porcini's* flavors kept exploding in my mouth, pungent, sweet, wild, smoky, and unforgettably good. And the wine. Thank you, Bacchus. And thank you, Candace, because she had asked the man at the store for a nice wine with *porcini*, and the man handed her a bottle of Brunello from nearby Montalcino—both names as familiar to us as baseball to a Martian—and it cost all of seven dollars in those days and turned out to be one of Italy's great wines. So we ate and we drank and the fire blazed, and the sun streamed in and we sank: deeper in love with Tuscany, deeper in love with life, and I would have happily given the three trillion or whatever Duillio was asking for his crumbling stable, except that I didn't have it. Without touching the tomatoes we ate the leftover squashed brie so we could sip more wine, then we went out while there was sun left, for a walk in Tuscany.

We walked, arm in arm, through the great cavern of oaks, and the wind, as it rose and fell, brought first a puff of warm air from the fields, than a draft of cool from the woods below. I was telling Candace about my morning's adventure and how we might have to settle for a trailer near Torino, but she kept gazing off among the trees, taking deep breaths of the forest air. Then she turned off into the woods. She came back with one hand behind her, and I thought, "God, not more *funghi!*" when she told me to close my eyes and open my hand. I did. "Now close it," she said. I did that too. A sensuous, crumbling velvet rubbed against my palm. "Smell it," she said. I did. It was an odor so sad, so thrilling, so reassuring, so exquisitely complete, as if all flowerings and all wiltings in history were in it. It was earth, from the forest floor.

The stone walls of the hamlet were golden in the low sun. The cow was no longer tethered in the chapel yard, but we heard its snorting from nearby, and the soft thud of its hoof on a solid floor. The wooden door to the small stable near the chapel was open, and from a chest-high opening in the loft above where a handmade wooden ladder led, an invisible hand pitched hay into the street. We stopped and watched. When there was a goodly little mound, the old man who had tended the smoldering fire the night before came out, and climbed with his pitchfork, *piano, piano*, down the uneven rungs. He looked up, saw us, and he smiled. It wasn't a smile of either surprise or slight embarrassment, nor the slightly hollow city smile that we had gotten used to, but a deep, heartfelt smile, full of expectation, that beguiling smile that children have, tugging at the wrapping of a present. It was a smile that we would see often through the years in the Tuscan countryside, the smile of men and women who had grown old finding life's greatest pleasures in the company of people: family, friends, neighbors, passersby. And now the old man with the pitchfork was meeting us, and his face shone, looking forward to the adventure.

"*Buongiorno,*" Candace and I said almost in chorus.

"*Buonasera,*" he responded, the smile still blooming.

"*Che animali ha Lei?*" she asked brazenly, pointing into the

gloom of the stable. The old man beamed at the chance of showing off his kingdom. *"Prego, prego. Venite,"* and he motioned broadly for us to go in. We went.

The stable was tiny. It had looked tiny from the outside, but
inside, with the thick stone walls consuming space, it looked like a
children's stage set. While Candace and the old man chatted softly, I, banished to silence, looked around. There was only the one
cow at the manger, who now, annoyed at the delay of her hay,
stomped and shuffled her great feet in the straw. Beside her was a
nanny with a pendulous udder that stroked the ground, and in the
corner opposite, fenced in by sheaves of corn, her sleepy eyelids
sagging, a brooding hen was draped over eggs that peeked from
below her wings. The place seemed timeless. Almost holy. If it had
been late December, I would have looked for Baby Jesus.

A rattle of gravel and the sound of a child's cheery yells
broke the spell. I went out. A little boy of about five was tearing
around on a tricycle, with a small box of chicken feed lashed onto
his rear axle, and behind him cackled a cloud of frantic chickens
who were trying to catch their dinner. His older sister chased him
with a rake, yelling *"Ti ammazzo! Ti ammazzo!"*—I'll kill you, I'll
kill you—and tried to hook his wheels. But the boy kept swerving
and she kept missing, whacking instead the poor, desperate chickens. I called out to Candace and they both came out. *"Nonno!
Aiuto! Prendilo!"* the girl yelled. But Grandpa wasn't about to help.
Not for all the rice in China. His smile had changed, the expectation turned to mischief, and he looked for all the world as if he'd
happily exchange a few days of his life for a last ride on that tricycle with the cloud of mad chickens fluttering behind.

The sun was falling. I nudged Candace and pointed to it.
The old man understood and we said our good-byes. We kept

retracing our steps on the road we had arrived on the day before—
a whole lifetime ago. We passed the Madonna with her jam jar of
flowers, and passed Bastardino, wandering down toward the cemetery where the cypresses were growing dark against the sky.
"Remember what David said about the Irish after he moved back
to County Limerick?" Candace mused. "That if this modern world
crumbled, the people there could go back three hundred years
without batting an eye. This place is the same, don't you think?
Eternal, in a way."

The sun slid low.

A pair of older ladies, square-shouldered and sturdy of limb,
dressed in skirts and coats and scarves for a respectful cemetery
visit, came toward us arm in arm. They bade us polite *Buonasera*s
but eyed us curiously. *"Ti ammazzo! Ti ammazzo!"* drifted from
afar.

At the cemetery, we slowed. We turned in. The cemetery
was surrounded by a man-high wall, the rusted iron gate held shut
by a chain. When I loosened the chain, the weight of the gate,
angled slightly inward, pulled me in, as a welcome, or a reminder
of mortality. There were flowers everywhere, and flickering electric
candles upon the graves—some under frosted glass the shape of a
flame, some in tiny bronze lanterns, others in miniature versions of
a dome.

The tombs themselves were simple travertine slabs; a small
piece under the upright headstone of the same pale, porous stone,
and a larger piece about four feet long, a sort of lid, over the rest.
And they were thin, these lids, no more than an inch, hence not
too heavy—for an average spirit in good shape—to slide silently

back, on the way out for a stroll in the silence of the night. Twilight was falling. Candace grew more curious and headed for the chapel that rose from the back wall. Not wanting to be alone, I followed. The older headstones had chiseled names, the newer ones embossed bronze letters, but almost all of them had a small photograph of the occupant below. Giuseppe Zamperini, big mustached farmer, gazed out at me. 1860–1939: good life. Angelo Magi, 1866–1944. Big ears, huge sunken eyes, long straight nose, hair cropped to the skull, chin as prominent as his giant cheekbones, long neck with a low white collar and tie. His wife beside him died the year after. A bunch of old crosses of wrought iron leaning against the wall in the corner. Giuseppe Brogi. Simple country face, with the inscription *"Uomo buono e laborioso."* And just past him *"Qui riposa* Agaliano Lucatti 1923–1987.*"* Honest face, thick eyebrows, wide open shirt collar, slightly furrowed forehead. And under the oval frame the last inscription, *"Amico di tutti."* Friend of all. My eyes fill. God knows why. The cypresses cast shadows much longer than their boughs.

A very old man I hadn't noticed before moved in the arcade whose tall wall is covered with square headstones. One is still open and I see the long deep hole. He tries to move a steel ladder leaning against the wall, but it's too heavy and he quits and ambles to a headstone, looks up, pokes about. It's a beautiful woman with gray hair and intelligent eyes. The old man hears me coming and looks up and there's that smile. "Can I help?" I say in English, motioning to bring the ladder. *"No, no, va bene così,"* he says, than asks instantly, "England?" "No," I say. "America." His eyes grow blazing bright. "America very good," he says. "I, wounded in war. America help me two years." What that means we don't know and can't ask. The old man looks up at the intelligent woman's grave and points. *"Mia moglie,"* he says, peacefully. My wife. She died four years before. Then he points at the empty hole next to hers, *"Questo è per me."* This is for me. And smiles. Someone, probably a relative, had left a pot of flowers. Candace touches the old man's arm, *"Ha già portato fiori per se stesso?"* The old man breaks into laughter and laughs and laughs, and his bent back almost straightens out with laughter. I ask Candace what on earth she said. "I asked if he had already brought flowers for himself."

"America very good," the old man says.

The tiny flames are flickering bright now. The sun is gone. We bid good-bye and we go. We're well outside the gate and around the wall when the old man again breaks into laughter. We walk fast in the twilight. *"Ti ammazzo! Ti ammazzo!"* floats on the still air.

"Tuscany very good," Candace says.

And that was the end of the first whole day.

5 ~ OH SO-LE MI-I-O

*T*he next morning I awoke full of apprehension. I stared at the ceiling of massive oak beams, the stringers of oak and the rough terra-cotta tiles between them, and although they were reassuring in their simplicity and strength, they personified a strangeness: a strange land, a strange people, and nothing but the unknown everywhere. In that early hour, few things seemed more frightening than burying our life's savings in a house near a town that until two weeks ago we didn't even know existed. How could I have been so naive? So impractical. Lying there, it was easy to think the worst. And the pillow beside me was empty—the voice of reason wasn't there to calm me.

I got up and opened the shutters. Tuscany hit me with the full force of her beauty. During the night, the fresh north wind had driven all moisture from the air, and beyond the pines, in that brilliant translucence, the layers of hills now stood out crystal clear, welcoming, comforting, as if nothing could ever go wrong with the world. Someone had brought two cows into the unfenced field below and tethered them on long ropes. As they ambled around the stakes driven in the ground, the ropes made perfect circles in the hay. Into that morning silence came a rustling from the woods across the road, and into the sunlight burst Candace, beaming, holding up a hand like the Statue of Liberty, yelling, *"Porcini!* I found my own *porcini."*

Over a steaming cappuccino and some fresh bread with plum jam thick as mud, I listened to Candace's joyous tales of *porcini* hunting. Then she went down to the insectorium to paint, and I to try to find a roof over our heads.

Monte San Savino was still quiet. The town gate yawned wide. It was too early for the stores to be open, so except for the street sweeper with his long, worn broom, the streets were empty. He worked with an easygoing motion, the twigs of his sweep lopsided with use, whooshing in even arcs over the stones. He stopped now and then to load bits of paper into his pushcart, or to stroke a cat lying in a window, or to cheer on a kid running late to school. When he reached a café, he parked his gear and got ready to go inside just as a gust of wind whipped some papers from his cart back into the street. I prepared myself for a violent string of Madonnas and saints in compromising positions, for Tuscan swearing makes all Italy blush, but the sweeper threw open his arms, looked up at the heavens and chided, *"È una cosa bella questa?"* Which means more or less, Now, was that nice? Then he calmly picked up the escaped papers, reincarcerated them, washed his hands at a nearby tap and vanished in the café. It seemed like perfect street theater, and over the years I learned that that's exactly what it was. Italians have somehow made an art of converting anger into laughter, or at least a joke, or at worst a rosary of creative swear words.

The most unforgettable example we had seen on the Amalfi coast the year before. The coast road etched in the cliffs above Positano is probably the narrowest, most harrowing and most stunning in all Italy. On the hairpin-curve bridges over gorges which slice the mountainside straight down to the sea, two cars seldom pass without one backing up. But two busses never pass, and when there is traffic, there is nowhere to back up to without somehow shifting at least twenty cars. We were in such a jam. Movement was impossible. Hope abandoned. Behind us people waved and yelled in frustration, and right behind me, a desperate taxi driver leapt savagely from his car, slammed the door so hard his car shook, his face wrung with venom, and I still cannot believe what happened to this day. The man whipped off his cap, and being from Sorrento—and I swear that this is true—broke into a passionate rendition of *"O So-o-ole Mi-i-io."*

Candace and I laughed until we cried. And from then on, whenever we had doubts about getting a place in Italy, remembering that moment always tipped the scales.

"Buongiorno, Scrittore," someone called out next to me. It was Neri. The habit of titles still persists in parts of Tuscany. So, instead of a surname, greeting and reference is often done using *professore*, or *architetto, avvocato*, or the more generic *dottore*, for which any turnip qualifies by scraping through four years of university. So anyway, I was stamped *scrittore* and that was that. *"Prendiamo un caffè,"* Neri suggested and I couldn't refuse: he had woven his arm in mine and moved me on.

Now I had been used to having coffee in Paris bistros, where engagements lasted eternities, filled with laments about past love affairs, or current love affairs, or future love affairs which could involve any human, bird or beast within the city limits. Not in Italy. Here coffee is not a social drink—it is a drug. It is not drank; it's mainlined. No sooner does the tiny espresso cup and saucer touch the counter than *whoosh*, in goes a quarter-pound of sugar, and *whoosh* the thing is downed in one gulp, and the caffeine is racing through your veins and you're ready to attack—literally—the world. So while I was still looking for the sugar, Neri had stirred, gulped, paid and was at the door waiting. Since I had not been given an asbestos liner for my throat, I had to smile at him and drink my brew sheepishly.

We went to his office where yesterday's smoke still fouled the air. He took from an old dresser a shoe box, whose contents looked decidedly more like a maiden aunt's girlhood letters than a reliable realtor's files. There were cards of odd sizes, scraps of paper, photographs, folded maps, torn cardboard bits, some keys with notes stuck through them, a small Italian-German dictionary, and two large purple dice. Neri was ready for anything. He rummaged through the junk, pulled out three odd bits, made a phone call and spoke so fast I couldn't get a word. Then he picked up the Italian-German dictionary and bid me follow him into the street once again.

"Tudei," he said in what he must have meant to be English, "one frend speek Inglish." And he waved his German dictionary. But Neri was no fool. He knew how to choose reinforcements. We ducked under the half-raised curtain of the pizzeria and I prepared my eyes for the blinding alabaster ankles. But instead there was a pair of long legs in high heels and dark stockings standing there before me and above them hovered Elena, dressed as if going dancing. I got uneasy. I took a deep breath. That was a mistake: Elena must have marinated herself overnight in perfume. We went out. We took the Lancia and began climbing up through curving terraces of olives, and more terraces of vineyards, and there in the pure sunlight with the most beautiful parts of Tuscany before me, Neri played his trump card: he handed me an old black-and-white photo of the most beautiful farmhouse in Tuscany. "Ve go," he said.

Almost all of Tuscany's farmhouses started much like a child's drawing of a house; a blocky building, a door, windows, and a chimney. The long outside staircase along the wall was normally the only thing to break the monotony. To some houses pieces were added through the centuries, as families grew or as the landlords got richer—a feudal system of landowners and peasants held much of Italy in its grip until the late 1940s—and it was these add-ons that made the houses interesting and unique. The add-on might have been a structure on the roof for raising pigeons, or for aging *prosciutto* in winter and *vinsanto* year round. At ground level it might have been a shed for hay, or a giant outside brick oven for baking bread, or arched stables for cows. In time of war they might have added a tower for defense—a rare jewel; in time of prosperity, a wing for children; in a fit of piousness, a chapel; or for great serenity, a walled garden. And on magically rare occasions, these stone structures of varied sizes, varied rooflines, and unique openings would, as if by a design that unfolded over centuries, form in the center, the most mysterious and comforting space of all, a courtyard. And this combination of architectural features created that rare house that had *movimento*. Movement. The farmhouse in the photograph had *movimento* to burn.

Now I was doubly uneasy. I opened the window and breathed deep to calm my senses, but the autumn fragrance of the countryside made me swoon the more. I kept looking back at the picture to make sure I wasn't dreaming, but the house was still there, *movimento* and all. After many hairpins we stopped, got out and headed uphill on a dirt trail where no one had passed since Napoleon left Elba. The trail was full of rocks and clumps of bush but Elena—who so far had not spoken a word in any language—didn't mind. She planted her high heels with expertise and weaved and bobbed herself among the stones.

Then we were there. We stood on an outcropping overlooking half of Tuscany. There were old fruit trees, a stone well and a pond and then the hill dropped precipitously, and across the great broad valley the snowy Apennines rimmed the horizon. Beyond the pond, woods fell languidly away, and to our right, a terraced olive grove sunk gradually from sight. The place had its own hilltop. You could withstand a siege here for a decade. It was definitely a place where a castle should have been. It was, at any rate, a place where *something* should have been—anything. But all around us were only trees and brambles and space.

Neri talked and the girl talked and for emphasis he now and then waved the German dictionary, and they both kept pointing ahead, there, there, at an enormous bramble mound, and I looked "there, there" until my eyes bulged from my head, until through the brambles I finally saw the most spectacular farmhouse in Tuscany. I went down to it. I walked all around, peeked in through the vines, checked against the photograph to ascertain my bearings, and I found it all. Everything was laid out just as in the photo, the arched walkway, the stables, the chapel and even the courtyard in whose center an ancient olive bloomed. It was all there. Except for one thing. The most spectacular farmhouse in Tuscany came up only to my knees. The rest was gone. I stood in shock.

I felt someone near me and I turned. It was Elena. She must
have sensed my disappointment at finding the house of my dream
not even a pile of rubble, and she looked at me kindly. Then she
explained slowly, but in clear English, that the owner had taken the
old house, stone by stone, and built his cows a new barn down the
road. I almost cried. I kept looking at the picture of that spectacular piece of architecture that had evolved in harmonious proportions over the centuries, then looked down at the remnants: some
ignoramus carts off six hundred years of history so his cows can shit
inside. I mumbled that they better guard Saint Peter's before someone hauls it off to add to his garage.

Twenty years ago, Elena explained, no one wanted these
houses. Some were torn down for material, others just collapsed,
and a few were even bulldozed by farmers who didn't want their
fields ruined by ruins; they wanted to reap one more sack of grain.
It was a poor country then, especially in these hills, and the people
needed everything to survive.

But, and here she cheered up, things have changed. Things
have changed to the other extreme. Old houses cannot be touched,
only rebuilt. Precisely as they were. And new houses can be built
on farmland only in rarest circumstances. But this land has *il dirit-
to,* the right, to rebuild the old house. No changes. And I could
take the stones from the same fields, use tree trunks from the same
woods, find old *tegole* and *coppe* for the roofs, and it would look
exactly like the old one.

I shuddered.

It wasn't just the cost—I couldn't even imagine how many
king's ransoms it would take to reconstruct what in fact had the
complexity of a small castle. What made me shudder was the loss
of an old place. All the things it had seen, the lives it knew. I don't

believe in ghosts or spirits, but upon entering an old house, built by hand, measured by eye, a feeling comes over me that I can't define. Perhaps it's all imagined instead of felt, I cannot say, but something calming sinks into me, and moments flicker before me from a thousand years of lives lived within those walls, laughter, tears, worries about drought, or a sick child, an old mother, a lean harvest. And the dreams. When they had a moment of repose in their slow but labored lives, what were their dreams? Leaning against that arch, staring through that gate, what did they hope for? Or long for? And on winter evenings, sitting on the small benches inside the yawning fireplace, close to the flames, what did they fear the most? And what made them laugh the most? In the stark Tuscan farmhouse that often had but a table with two benches, some beds and little more, what tiny precious things did they place with reverence in the tiny niches hollowed in the walls? And what about the abyss of the night? The abyss of those enormous moonless, unilluminable nights, with the candles extinguished and the fires down to coals, when the only light in the world was from the stars, when all earth, all fields, all woods were dark and darker shadows? What did they feel then? What did they think? About the dark. Or the stars. Or themselves. In all that silence. Those feelings, those moments, were lost. Forever.

When I looked up, Elena was gathering small plants from the crevices of a stone wall. I went over. She looked up as open as a child, and showed me a clump of what looked like geranium leaves, and little, round, green buds. *"Capperi,"* she said, and I recognized the capers. "This other I don't know the name but it is very good when you have *bronchite*." I found later that most Tuscans possess an almost wondrous amount of knowledge about herbs. They have a love of nature not only because it soothes their soul, but because it helps to heal their bodies. So they feel at home in the countryside, among friends. And among *funghi.* Because right then from behind the mound of brambles Signor Neri came, with a full paper bag held up in his arm, and said bashfully, *"Funghi."*

I told him and the girl translated, that this hilltop was magnificent but I didn't want to build a new old house. We have those in Disneyland. They laughed. *"Al prossimo,"* To the next, Neri good naturedly said, *"Qui, non ce n'è più di fungi."*

We drove east. I sat behind Neri and, now and then, glanced at the girl. Her calm helped to lift my spirits. This time we talked. Neri asked questions and the girl interpreted. They were questions about what I really wanted. What sort of house, how big, how much land, how many neighbors. I told them we lived for two years on a thirty-two-foot sailboat, so size was not an issue. But it had to be very private, with a few acres of land—a few olives, some grapes, a bit of woods—and just as important I wanted to see those blazing Tuscan sunsets. And it had to be old. And preferably habitable. At least a bit more so than Duillio's three rooms above and stalls below.

We were still in high country, and the countryside kept changing as the road rose and fell, from woods, to fields, to olive groves and back to woods again. We passed a small old farmhouse that butted on the road. It was still lived in. There were curtains on the windows, chickens on the stairs, laundry sailing on a line in the breeze, a few flowers in corners and nooks, and a great rambling vegetable garden. And the earth all around the house was tamped hard from daily use. The house was in fine shape although untouched for decades. "Something like this would be perfect," I exclaimed.

Signor Neri agreed instantly. *"Ideale,"* he said. *"Tante piante di castagne."*

"Lots of what?" I asked the girl.

"*Castagne*," she repeated, pointing at the big trees with pointed leaves that ringed the house. "I don't know the English."

I raced through my edible plants in the French and English but found nothing that sounded close, when an old Hungarian word jumped in: *Gesztenye,* the most beloved dessert of my childhood. Chestnut purée, with rum and whipped cream. Every birthday my dad would take me to a little bistro by Népliget Park and I would spend an hour eating a cup of it, almost invisible spoonfuls at a time to make it last, combining just the right amount of whipped cream and purée. *Gesztenye.* Here! Trees of it! Cup hell. I'll eat fruit-bowls at a time. My spirits flew again. I got excited. And I liked Signor Neri more with every hour. How can you not like a man who judges houses not by size, prestige or location, but by what you can eat from the earth around it.

"*A vendere questa casa?*" I asked, pointing back.

"Impossible." The girl replied on her own. "They are *contadini.* Farmers. Just like the dead; they never leave the ground." And she laughed.

We flew around a corner and into a wall of sheep straddling the road. We braked. They leapt. We skidded. They bleated. Neri said a quick rosary of Madonnas, leapt out of the car and roared "Bindi! Bindi!"

"*Che c'è?*" somebody yelled back. Then a very short and very wall-eyed shepherd appeared from a hut. Neri stood in front of him and yelled for a while. The shepherd stared at Neri with one eye, while the other roamed casually about counting sheep. Then the shepherd went to his hut and brought back three small gray balls of something and handed it to Neri. Neri gave him some money. Then they said good-byes. Neri came back, Bindi scattered his sheep from the road and we drove on. Neri reached back and handed me a ball.

"*Pecorino,*" the girl said. "Cheese of sheep. Aged four months in cave."

I thanked him profusely.

We dropped down into the broad Valdichiana, an immense valley that spreads east to where the Apennines stand snowcapped. Until the eighteenth century the valley was swamp and bog, then the Austrians drained it and made it into one of the most fertile small valleys in Italy. It was like entering a different world. The olives, woods and vines gave way to vast fruit orchards and plowed fields. Instead of hamlets there were enormous, blocky farmhouses made of brick. I asked why the houses were so huge, compared to the ones in the hills. "The land is rich here. It feed more people. People of hills very poor," Elena said.

I asked, not too enthusiastically, if the house we were about to see was in the valley. No, I was told, in the foothills near Cortona. I cheered up. I remembered Cortona from my inquiries. A perfect medieval town carved in the hillside. City of art, birthplace of Luca Signorelli. Started by the Etruscans, savaged by Arezzo in some medieval century. But mostly I remember the photo of its irregularly shaped *piazza* with a monumental stone staircase, upon which were clustered Cortona's citizens, sitting in the sun, being social. I remember feeling envious at that sight. The ease. The belonging. And now Cortona hovered ahead in all her splendor. Serene, dignified. And we kept rising. We were among small, shallow hills, miniature versions of those around Monte San Savino.

Neri began to talk and the girl translated. The house had six hectares—fifteen acres. One acre of vines, two of olives, a bit in fruit, some fields, and a bit of woods. It sounded much too good. I dreaded to see what horror the house would be. I imagined the worst: no house at all or a mobile home on blocks. Neri must have sensed this and said that the house had been completely renovated the year before with "*gusto perfetto.*" Perfect taste. The price was at our very upper limit but if we sold the Matra and got a mule, and if I could get an advance on a future book—God knows about what. The day grew hot. Then we swung onto a dirt road and a few minutes later turned between stone columns of a gate.

And then I saw the house.

I think I died. It was, without doubt, the Second Most Beautiful Farmhouse in Tuscany. And it was all *there!* Way past my knees! All the way up to its gorgeous, ancient, terra-cotta roof! With a luxuriant mature garden all around it. The house had two floors and a little tower. On ground level two broad archways fronted a *loggia*, with great terra-cotta vases of oranges and lemons. A pair of centuries-old doors, worn in places where hands had worked the sliding lock, formed the entrance. We went in.

It seemed like a medieval castle. The house was built into a gentle hill, and the stone floors of different levels followed the grade. Massive brick arches and brick columns supported the floor above. Light poured in through scattered windows and lay in shafts and pools. The level to the right was for reading; easy chairs, a Persian rug, a huge niche with shelves of books hollowed in the wall. To the left was a long, medieval dining table hewn from wood as thick as beams. Along it, similarly massive wooden benches. The kitchen lay ahead. The rear wall was a walk-in fireplace, with benches and iron hardware to hold pots and roasting meat. There was a small brick structure, stove height, with openings in its sides to insert glowing coals, and round holes above for pots. The fire was down, and I asked Neri if the owners lived here. He told me no. It was rented to a Swiss *industrialista* for his holidays.

A broad stairway made of planks led to the floor above. The room there must have been the old kitchen, for it had a fireplace as big as ours in Palazzuolo Alto, and doors opened from it into well-restored bedrooms and new baths. Everything was perfect. Everything was in *"gusto perfetto,"* just as Neri had said.

Then we headed down out to the garden. I didn't notice the strange smell until I was halfway down the stairs. Past the lemon and orange trees the smell hit me again, along with a brilliant reflection of sunlight on steel. Less than a mile away, rising from the bucolic Tuscan countryside, in the middle of that perfection, was a small hell in paradise. Poking its giant smokestack to the sky, with stainless steel bands that reflected the sun, was a giant fertilizer plant. I died again. This time an ugly death.

I had dreamt for a year about the perfect Tuscan house, and now, no matter how I tried, I just could not fit a fertilizer plant into those dreams. Neri and the girl came toward me looking disconcerted. I didn't know whether he was reacting to my face or the lack of *funghi* around the house. He asked me what I thought and I answered pointing to the smokestack, *"Troppo industriale."* Neri agreed. *"La nostra zona è molto più bella. Torniamo a casa."* Our area is nicer. Let's go home.

The Swiss industrialist came up the drive in a Mercedes the size of a barge. He greeted us in polite, flawless English. I told him this was the most beautiful house I had seen for sale. Then we left. The next day I heard he had bought the place. I guess some people have more fertilizer in their dreams than others.

By the time we got back to Monte San Savino, the streets

were full of life. The cafe had two tables out in the *piazza*, and the shopkeepers put chairs and stools and crates against the walls, and sat and chatted, and stored up the sun's heat for the winter. We went to Neri's office and he made two phone calls but to no avail. The Tuscan farmhouse of my dreams was nowhere to be found. At least not in the hills around Monte San Savino.

I thanked him profusely, thanked Elena too, and headed home. From out in the street I took one last look at the brown saint in the window, his brown cassock, the smoke brown background, his youthful white face, the graying skull in one hand and white lilies in the other. Today he seemed content—and why not—he already had himself a place in Tuscany. He could take time to contemplate life, death, and eternity until hell froze over. I began to grow fond of him. I went back in and asked the price of that beautiful old painting. Neri laughed. Old? It was practically new. Didn't I see the date? He went and yanked it irreverently from its place, dusted it roughly with a rag, and held it in the smoky light. In the bottom right-hand corner in delicate numbers stood "1865."

"Vedi? Appena un secolo."

"See," the girl translated, "barely a century." To them the thing was a joke; almost new. To me it was the oldest thing I ever had a chance to own.

"Quanto costa?" I sheepishly inquired.

"Centomila," Neri said.

I took a moment to figure out the zeros. When I did, I thought I heard wrong, I must have. But by then Neri had his old adding machine humming, yanked down the lever, tore off the bit of tape and handed it to me.

"Centomila lire," he said again. *"Settantacinque dollari."*

I thought he was crazy. Seventy-five dollars for an antique

oil painting the size of a small window?

"*Troppo?*" Neri asked. Too much?

I looked at his face tried to see if some malady had struck him, but he was the same old Neri I had known.

"*Troppo poco,*" I said. Not enough.

"O.K." Neri laughed. "Seventy *dollari.*"

I had to stop him before he changed his mind. "*Venduto,*" I said. And dug feverishly in my pocket and gave him my set-aside spare dollars. Then I gingerly took my saint from his hands, slipped him under my arm, and said my good-byes. Out in the street, I couldn't help but hold him up for another look. In the sun he didn't seem so sad, just musing on that old skull. I stood like a fool in the middle of the street staring at my saint. A lady with a cotton net full of groceries peeked at it, smiled and said, "*Che bello,*" crossed herself and went on. It was then I noticed a small white ribbon painted at the bottom, and over it a name: S. Filippo. I had my own saint. Coming home with me. I no longer felt a stranger in Tuscany.

The church bells tolled one. The last store shutters came down, the last keys turned, and the street emptied as if for an air raid. I went out under the town gate, and there in the empty park I heard a raspy, amplified voice coming nearer and nearer. Then a Cinquecento rounded the corner with an ancient loudspeaker lashed to its roof, blaring, "*Circo, Circo, Circo! Circo Orfeo!*" then an endless stream of words. Tied to the back was a billboard of a circus-lady riding a tiger. A little girl leaned out from a second-story window and waved. When the car was gone, she waved to me. I waved back. Then I held up S. Filippo and shook him from side to side and had *him* wave too. The little girl let out a gleeful laugh that only little girls can make when the circus is coming to town.

6 ~ BOAR!

We wound homeward, San Filippo and I, up through the hills. Just before the pass I caught a little school-bus chugging around the curves. I stayed behind and realized, to my surprise, how carefree it felt to be driving so slowly, gazing around, dreaming, wondering.

The hillside around the house was bathed in lustrous light. The cows had each eaten down a ring of hay, and now, contented, stared as I arrived. I called out for Candace to come and meet somebody. She came, paintbrush in hand. She liked San Filippo, skull and all, and we took him into her studio to clean him up. The canvas she had been working on was reveling in color. In a pearly sunset were voluptuous hills like naked bodies, and naked bodies redolent of the hills. And there was a blue stream winding and a pond with a face in it staring at the sky. And the colors: bottomless layers of them, as if centuries of sunsets and centuries of lives shimmered below their surface. As an art historian wrote years later, "It invites us to dream." I told her how marvelous it was. "Thank you," she smiled, "but I'd rather go hunt *funghi.*"

Then we ate. I remember few gastronomic moments in my life with as much clarity as that one. I recall my mother's chicken soups and some of her baking; a bowl of mussels cooked with shallots and white wine in a bar full of fishermen in Brittany; a New Year's banquet of ten courses in Arles; our thirteenth anniversary dinner at Relais Louis XIII in Paris with thirteen roses on the table; and the lunch that day. It started simply enough with some aged *prosciutto,* as dry as beef jerky, and that little sheep cheese from Bindi, and a peppery wild-boar sausage, and crusted fresh bread, and the Brunello that by now we were drinking like table wine. But the surprise came afterwards with the tomatoes. Candace had asked for olive oil at the hamlet's store, and the owner took her down to his *cantina* where a big earthen jar was hiding in the cold, and ladled some thick creamy oil into a jar for preserves. So we spooned some of that over the sliced tomatoes, and chattered away about Neri and his house-no-house, and then we took a bite. And fell silent. We looked at each other. What kind of flavors do these tomatoes *have?* They tasted peppery and bittersweet, and tangy with a complexity that burst as it passed over your tongue. Then we realized it wasn't the tomatoes at all, but the opaque green olive oil that we'd poured over them. We poured some more. We dipped bread in it. We spooned it. We dipped a carrot in it. We dipped our fingers in it. We licked the forks. And we moaned like kids let loose in a pastry shop. It was our first encounter with hill-grown, stone-pressed Tuscan olive oil. One of God's great creations—now that we press our own, we use a quart a week. We finished with some apples, then, after a job well done, we went for a walk in the hills. I got suspicious when Candace stuffed a folded paper bag into her pocket. "No more *funghi,*" she said. "I promise."

We walked back though the hamlet enveloped in after-

pranzo repose, and headed east, where, we were told, the woods hid a small, walled castle. We followed a rutted road, then, when it swerved too far north, we left it and kept eastward on the edge of a plowed meadow. There were no fences to make us feel unwelcome; the rolling hills, the fields and woods beckoned with open arms.

The open country is one of Tuscany's great charms. Rare are fences that delineate what one owns—a very few exist to hold in sheep or horses—so, for the lovers of long walks, the country is paradise. And the small dirt tracks that wind and swoop, so intimate and untravelled, stir in you the sense that something wonderful and unforeseen may lie around the bend. That sense was even stronger cutting through the land. The raw, coarse clumps of fresh-plowed earth kept us attentive at each step. We didn't talk. There were few sounds, only birds and the wind whispering through the pines. We followed a path into a stand of ancient oaks. The sun's rays danced far above us in the boughs and fell to the forest floor only now and then. Beside the path, every few feet, the leaves were oddly bunched—something had been digging, rooting up the ground. The path narrowed and descended. We rustled through the leaves. The air was cool and biting in the hollow. There was a smell of savage wilderness. *"Funghi,"* Candace whispered. I didn't say a word. The smell was no *funghi*. *Funghi* don't dig up the ground.

Candace put out an arm and motioned me to stop. I did. She pointed into the gloom ahead. Something moved. I thought a small wolf or a fox, but then the beast made a sudden turn toward us; it was a dog. "You know what that is?" Candace whispered.

"A dog," I said. "Why are we whispering?"

"No, Future Tuscan Land Owner, that is not *a* dog, that is

the dog. The most precious dog in all of Tuscany. You know what it's doing in the woods?"

"Probably the same thing as the bear."

"It is digging. You know why?"

"From a sense of common decency?"

"From a sense of uncommon sophistication. It is digging for," and she formed the word with pure joy, "truf-fles."

I didn't say so, but I had to admit she might be right. There were after all signs of digging along the path, and that was a very intelligent, well-cared-for little dog. But where was the owner? He looked at us in a most friendly fashion but went back to sniffing the path with a professional's dedication.

"Come on," Candace whispered. "It's going to find us the truffle of our lives."

The dog moved cautiously, with a controlled agitation. It sniffed one side of a path then the other, wondering off the path then back on it again, then went to an enormous oak tree with a big hole rotted in its trunk. He sniffed around its base. Candace gave me a nudge. "Watch," she whispered. "Truffles attach themselves to the roots of oaks." But the dog lost interest there, and went back down the path keeping his head at a vigilant angle near the ground. We followed. I don't know why to this day but we kept as quiet as we could, stepping carefully on the softly rustling leaves as if afraid to rouse the subterranean fungus from its sleep. The smell of savage wildness tumbled through the air. In a burst of sun, a small rocky cliff rose to our left, and below it, a ledge of broom and bunched coarse pampas grass grew on the sunny ground. The dog growled softly, then, his agitation getting the better of him, went at a faster pace,.

"Don't lose him now," Candace warned, "he's excited. He

can smell a truffle at fifty yards." The dog sped up again, then, caution and vigilance cast to the wind, lowered its head and dove at full speed down the path. We ran. It flew with fury then lunged through the air and threw itself at something large and black sleeping curled up in the grasses. The black thing jumped. It gave a violent squeal and leapt up in the air. Its fur and thin legs shimmering in the light, it landed running and counterattacked the dog; plowed into him and threw him like a rag doll at the cliff. The dog had pride. He bared his teeth and lunged, and the black thing turned and—ran directly at us.

"Boar! Boar!" I roared and grabbed Candace, who stood rooted to the ground. We ran. We ran at full speed back on the only path, with the terrified boar thundering behind, and the sonavabitch dog, who didn't know a truffle from a turd, yelping and howling at full speed after him. They were closing in. We were losing our lead at every step and with but ten yards left Candace yelled out, "Climb!" We threw ourselves like cartoon cats against the cliff and scrambled, kicked and clawed, and with all that effort ended up about four feet off the ground. But that was enough. The boar and the dog rushed by below us. We hung on until the dog's yelp faded and the warm silence returned. Candace had a scratch on one cheek and a mischievous grin. "Well," she said, "have you ever seen a bigger truffle in your life?"

～

We were lost. We had no idea how far the truffle hunt had taken us, so we turned back sweating and laughing, sometimes snorting from laughing, then laughing at the snorting, beating the bushes with sticks, stomping our feet, whistling, hollering, anything to keep the boar away. We were crossing the woods of the hollow oak when Candace stopped and pointed among the trees. "Look," she began, but I clutched her lapels, pulled her close and said with glaring eyes, "If you utter the word 'truffle,' I'll stuff you in the tree."

"Chestnuts," she whispered, her eyes glowing with mischief. "Edible." Those were holy words. She knew it. "You love me?" she said.

"Show me the chestnuts first."

She did. My God. I had never seen a live chestnut before. There they were all over the ground, with their soft furry shells opened wide and they peeking at us. We gathered. Me like a madman. I was stunned by my own reaction. I had never picked anything edible that grew wild in my life. I fished from our sailboat—although Candace always caught the fish—but just to wander and find something to eat to stay alive, that rekindled a flame from long ago, something from before the dawn of man. We filled up the paper bag, then I filled up my jacket pockets, then my pants pockets, then I waddled like an overstuffed doll westward through the woods. The sun was low; a solemnity hung like haze among the trees. Then I heard a comforting sound, a melodious voice on the evening wind, *"Ti ammazzo!"*

We were near home.

~

We had no whipping cream or rum to make the chestnut puree of my childhood birthdays, but Candace found in her studio an old tin frying pan rusted to perfection, with concentric circles of small holes drilled carefully in its bottom. Our hand-gathered chestnuts would be roasted over coals. But we were out of kindling. There was a nice pile of wood stacked beside the house, kept dry by a beat-up piece of corrugated tin, but the few bits of kindling that had been there we had used, so in the last gleam of twilight, while Candace chopped vegetables to concoct a soup, I went into the woods to gather more. The air had an autumn bite, and tufts of ground fog wafted in the valley. The hills were silent. I walked softly in the woods picking up fallen twigs and branches, some light as a feather from old rot, and now, alone, gathering sticks to build a fire, I felt that flush of primeval pleasure again. With only the woods full of shadows around me, I sloped my shoulders, hung my arms, bent my gait, and slouched and ambled in comfortable beastly ease. When I came upon a stick or twig I grunted softly, a guttural sound of joy, and that made the pleasure all the finer. Then I discovered cones.

I had entered into a clump of pines and, looking to the side, I stepped upon a cone, large and round; it cracked with a brittle sound. I reached down. The cone had fallen long ago, the scales, hard and woody, curled with dryness. I took off my jacket, laid it on the ground and filled it up. Then with the twigs under one arm and the bundle over my shoulder, I loped and grunted contentedly home.

I went into the kitchen to show my mate what a provider she had. She was delighted. Candace is always generous with her delight. But as I began to lay the cones in the fireplace she shrieked. I turned. "Can you believe this?" she asked, and between her fingers held up something small and white.

"Truffles?" I tried.

She smiled with understanding. "Pine nuts, Chum. *Pignoli.* Twenty bucks a pound."

"I knew that all the time," I said. "What kind of gatherer do you take me for?"

So we started the fire with twigs, sat face to face on the hearth and, with the aid of two round stones, we crushed the cones and extracted the slippery little critters the size of husked sunflower seeds. When our soup was ready and the pine nuts mixed into a spinach salad, I put two dozen chestnuts in the riddled frying pan, spaced them nicely the way I had seen the vendors do on Fifth Avenue in winter, then we sat down by the fire, and began our peaceful meal.

We were finishing our soup, listening to the silence, when the war broke out. Right there in the kitchen. "Bam!" the first cannonade exploded beside me. A fistful of shrapnel whistled past my ears. Bam, bam!! We ran. We covered our heads with our hands and flew out of the kitchen. Bam, bam, bam! the cannons roared. We stood shell-shocked in the hallway. Kabam!! A giant blast and the shrapnel scattered at our feet. I stared at Candace. She looked back sheepishly. "Chestnuts," she whispered. "Edible."

The chestnuts roasting in their husks had become little bombs, and now, one by one, they were trying to blow away the house. My stare became murderous. "First truffles and now this." I hissed. "What next? You gonna poison us with *pignoli*?" Bam! Bam!

"Oh my lord," Candace cried. "My *pignoli!*" And she pulled her shirt over her face and dove back into the battle, then ducked back out with her body wrapped protectively over the salad bowl.

"This gathering bullshit is dangerous," she blurted. "No wonder cavemen took up hunting."

Bamm!!!

It was time for manly action. I glanced around for protection. I saw a basket hanging from a beam. I turned it upside down and pulled it over my head. Then I headed into the midst of the exploding inferno. Shrapnel flew but I kept on toward the fire. When near the flames I waited for a "Bam" then, on the absurd premise that the next one wouldn't come for a while, I grabbed the frying pan, ran to the window and threw the whole exploding mess back into the primal forest where it bloody well belonged.

And that, praise the Lord, was almost the end of the third day.

Except that we ate the spinach and *pignoli* salad that tasted bittersweet like dreams come true, and went so very well with the Brunello. Then we gathered the larger pieces of shrapnel from the floor and, with our fingernails, dug out the still warm bits of chestnut from the shells. They tasted wonderful.

7 ~ HOUSES OF HORROR

*A*nother morning and still no house. But we weren't discouraged. Joyce—our contact for the rented house—had invited us for lunch, and assured us that there was life after Neri, because she had a friend who knew someone, who knew someone who might . . . etcetera.

Her house was down a bouncy, rocky road. Notched into the hillside, it was surrounded by an olive grove, with a castle peeking at it from the woods above: an old, unpretentious farmhouse, dream-size. An ancient oak shaded it with a child's swing dangling from a bough.

Joyce's house was wonderfully cozy. The stables below had been converted for people, but the ceiling remained low and the interior spaces, on varied levels, small—the front room held a baby grand piano and some built-in settees and that's all. But that center of Tuscan life, the kitchen, was long and had a fireplace in a corner. Its table was set and the sun poured in through the windows from a small meadow. The three rooms upstairs, with beamed and sloping ceilings, were perfect for sleeping.

The schoolbus honked on the hill, and out came her four-year-old, dark-haired Francesco, rumbling down the road kicking stones. While his Mom finished lunch, he showed us the fields. He knew every bush, every tree. He showed us olives that were turning dark with ripeness, showed us *finocchio,* fennel, that he had to pick for lunch, two bird's nests hidden in the deep dark of a thicket, and where he planned to build a fort in a rootcellar in the hill. I looked around with envy. What wouldn't I give to have lived there as a child.

During lunch we of course talked about houses. She had a friend who knew of some and would take us around that afternoon. The friend was young, brawny and jolly. As if on a timer, she broke into laughter once a minute. To fill the spaces, she talked, thank God in English.

The first house was nearby. It was not exceptional but it had beautiful long views, was old and livable, lacking only central heating and refined plumbing. What it didn't lack was a huge transmission tower bigger than Mr. Eiffel's right before its door. The owner, a loud *contadino,* assured me that in almost no time we would grow used to its presence. "Yes," I agreed, "just as soon as we go blind." Jolly girl laughed.

The second house was to the north toward Florence and we took some peacefully meandering roads to get there. It was an eighteenth-century villa surrounded by a shady park. It had a languor-inducing sunroom, a library, and the owner—a most gracious older lady—would even include some antique rugs and furniture. I walked around the house full of suspicion, on the lookout for fertilizer plants, refineries and state prisons, but there was only pristine countryside all around. We gulped. We had lovely tea in the garden in the sun. Then the wind changed, and instead of the birdsong and silence that had filled the afternoon until then, there rose the steady roar of the hidden freeway below the hill. We tried to hide our mortification as we said our good-byes. Jolly girl laughed.

The third house was near the medieval hill town of Lucignano. It was in the valley, and we could see its lonely tower ringed by cypresses from a distance. It was of perfect size, renovated with great care by an architect from Rome who preserved all the original spaces, openings and ancient material. And it came furnished. Even forks and knives. And around it the valley was pristine, vineyards, wheat fields, a stream behind grass-covered dikes, some woods in a dale, and no hill below or behind which some horror could be lurking. And the views from its tower captured the Apennines in the east, a fortress town on Lake Trasimeno in the south, and unimpeded sunsets to the west. We sat down at the kitchen table to iron out details of the by now inevitable sale. Then the earth moved. The windows rattled and lamps jiggled and a jet of sound shattered the air as if a bullet-train were screaming under the garden at two hundred miles an hour. Which it was.

Jolly girl laughed. Candace looked ready to run her through with a fork.

~

We quit.

We decided to give up house hunting because we were no good at it, and do instead what we do best: nothing. Be tourists for a day. Now *that* pumped life into my tired soul. Still full from lunch, we decided on a light dinner: roasted chestnuts and wine. We're no fools. This time we sliced each chestnut with a knife to let the murderous gases make good their escape. It worked. We got to stay in the kitchen. And the chestnuts roasted their little selves to perfection.

While we ate, we indulged in one of life's inexplicably great pleasures—looking at a map. We spread our *Istituto Geografico* map of Tuscany out on the kitchen table, pulled down the old glass lamp on a sliding cord until it hovered just above us, and instantly, as if it were some mysterious place we had never seen, began dreaming about spending a day touring Tuscany. How a few squiggly lines crisscrossing a splotchy green background can fire the imagination, I'll never understand, but for me it seems to happen every time. I stared at that map. I followed the twisting lines of dirt roads to where civilization ended and sorcery began, where perched on windy bluffs or huddled in shaded ravines were minuscule villages in tiny, barely legible script: Nusenna, Fietri, Duddova. My imagination flew. I was in streets of towns I'd never heard of, discovering ruins forgotten even by locals, walking up through a meandering stream to grottos of a necropolis untouched since the Etruscans. I was drawn into the emptiest part of the map: Zancona, Poggioferro, L'Abbandonato, drawn into the dark of Tuscany.

"And where will we have lunch?" Candace broke into my reverie.

I looked up. She was standing there armed to the teeth with her touring bibles: the Michelin Guides, Green and Red. She was, of course, right. We had learned from long experience. We opened up the books. We had done the same thing every Sunday that year we lived in Paris. We would find in the Green Guide some cultural wonder within an hour's or so drive, like Chartres cathedral, or a monastery, or a chateau. Then we would find in the Red Guide a restaurant with a red R, which meant exceptional food at low prices, where we could stuff ourselves. Although not quite in that order. The truth is that we looked in the Red Guide *first,* found a red R, and *then* we checked the Green Guide for culture in the neighborhood. But it worked out fine. We would leave at a reasonable hour, arrive by ten thirty, spend two hours touring the cathedral, museum, or architectural wonder, have lunch, then back for more culture, then go home.

Once.

I think we did that once.

The rest of the Sundays, I would go down for fresh croissants and fresh milk, then we would sip *cafés au lait,* leave in a late fury and arrive at the red R in the nick of time for lunch. We would eat at indulgent length, amble, stuffed and wined, to the cultural etcetera, try to focus with fuzzy eyes as they rushed us through before closing, *then* we would go home.

So Candace browsed the guides, cross-referred and back-referred and finally pointed much closer than I had wandered. "Abbey of Mont Oliveto Maggiore, founded in 1313. In an area of great isolation, beautiful church, stunning cloister, works by Della Robbia, Signorelli and Sodoma. *And*—what a coincidence—there is a fine small restaurant in the abbey's guard tower, with a terrace for dining. I think I'm in love." And she looked it. Then lightning struck.

The night turned blue-white. The hills were bright as day. A colossal thunder rocked the sky and the windows rattled in homage. The lights went out. We felt our way to the loggia for a look. The wind, which had turned to the south during the afternoon tea, was blasting ferociously through the landscape and the pines. The walk was littered with cones. The moon poked through morose, wind-whipped clouds, but a strange red haze hung before it, like a harvest moon. But duller. The air was warm. Like August.

Another blade of lightning slashed the sky, this time more distant, and it too was paled and reddened by the veil. The wind slammed a shutter with violence against a wall, and we stumbled around in the dark to find it. Then we retreated to the fire. The sky had become a tumult; the moon was on the run. Rain pelted in streams against the windows. When lightning exploded, we saw rivers of water gurgling down the road. When we went to bed, the rain tapped on the clay tiles overhead, and the wind and thunder shook the whole dark world.

"Strange," Candace whispered, "how we think of storm and rain as a lack of good weather. A lack. But there is so much to them. So much to feel when they close you in."

It rained all night.

~

At dawn, the sky was alight with a low red haze. The rain had eased to a drizzle and the sky was clearing but the haze remained. I stoked the dying embers of the fire and put on cones to rekindle the flames. No longer sleepy, I sat down to read. The light kept getting stronger, but only a stronger red. I looked out at the Matra and stared in dumb surprise. I had expected it to be clean from the rain, but instead it was spotted and streaked with a film of mud. I went out. A reddish dust had caked over it, and the dust packed thick in the corner of the windshield. It felt as fine as talcum. I looked around for a source—a field, the road, the old mortar between the stones, but everything there was white clay. There was no red anywhere. Except in the sky.

There was a grunting sound from the road, and the two pigs appeared, and a few steps behind came the Angel of the Key. She said a soft *buongiorno* and I replied in kind. I ran my hand over the car and showed her the caked red dust it collected, and shrugged my shoulders to show my questioning. She smiled. She smiled and her eyes widened in a look of mystery and she pointed guardedly at the sky. Then she said very softly, "*Afrika.*"

8 ~ EVIL WOMEN
IN THE MONASTERY

After breakfast we packed the emergency cheese and wine and a blanket—one never knows when one might need a nap in a meadow—then we washed *Afrika* from the Matra and headed out into the hills of Tuscany.

At Il Cacciatore, we turned south and kept along the pine-shrouded ridge, past wondrous ruins dominating promontories, then descended into a valley where horses ran in rain-soaked fields. Here the paved road ended and we slowed down in the mud. Plowed fields and woods alternated, and old farmhouses—still lived in—were set back from the road with haystacks, tractors, dunghills, and wet cows steaming in the sun. The red haze had moved on and the sky glowed blue and the sun danced on the puddles.

We went slowly. The winding road imposed a rhythm of its own. Some instinct reined me, slowed me to the clip-clop of a mule. The curves, the dips, the blind and narrow hairpins, dug and filled by gnarled hands a thousand years before, caressed us, bid us linger. We looked unhurriedly about, down the shadowy stream-beds with their rumbling waters; into the autumn forest where beads of rain hung like diamonds on the leaves; into the bustling barnyard morning where the chickens pecked at what the rain had torn loose from the dunghill, and a burly farmer and his smaller father tilted a two-wheeled wood-cart up to dry. The father, hearing our motor, turned his head, lifted an arm to shield his eyes from the low sun, and looked at us with that old, expectant smile.

Years ago the clip-clop on the road would have meant a neighbor or friend or a rare traveler passing by. Years ago the clip-clop would have slowed here, and even the traveler would have stopped, visited, chatted, commiserated about the *maledetta* rain, the *porca puttana tempesta,* the red *fango* that some fiend had sent from *Afrika,* and he would have helped, unasked, to pull the cart from the mud onto the paving stones to keep dry rot from the wheel a little longer. But we, with our windows closed, rolled anonymously by. And felt a lack.

~

We crossed the flat valley and climbed again. On a small rise, a castle tower burst out of the woods. A rusted sign read San Gimignanello. We stopped and searched the guide book to no avail. We thought omission of such a jewel an editorial error, but in the days that followed we came across castles, *palazzi* or small abbeys almost every mile, unmentioned, unknown, utterly mysterious.

We squeezed through the town gate of Asciano then out again, and back into pristine countryside, rising. At the top of a ridge the vista ahead was so utterly striking that I pulled the Matra into an open pasture and we got out to look. An improbably romantic landscape unfolded before us. Endless waves of rolling hills rippled westward to the mountains. And over the gentle hills and between them, everything meandered: streams, woods, groves, vineyards, ponds, undulating plowed fields, all following subtle changes in the slopes. On a hilltop stood a *palazzo* with its chapel, surrounded by clumps of giant cypresses and its cluster of dependent buildings. A vineyard of widely spaced, ancient vines, each the size of a fruit tree, fell into the valley. On steep slopes were patches of wood, a thicket, for birds to nest, pheasants to roost, foxes to burrow.

Beside us on a plowed, bare knoll, a great bowered pine stood alone against the sky. Left to stand by generations, perhaps for shade, perhaps for beauty, it appeared in that tremulous light as perfect an expression of enduring faith as any bell tower or steeple has ever been. And in the distance below the pine, scattered in the enormous tranquil vastness, rising on sun-flooded solitary knolls, ancient farmhouses, abandoned, ruined, beckoning, summoning. My throat tightened with greed.

"There's got to be something there," I said hoarsely to Candace. "I bet if we go down there we'll find something to buy."

"You know," she started pensively, "somebody once said, 'Man was born to live, *not* to prepare for life.'"

"Who said that?"

"Some Russian. Who else but a Russian would dare say a thing like that? So remember the thirteenth-century abbey, with spectacular works of art for lunch by someone's Granny in the kitchen. Drive on, James."

We drove. The road was empty. Since we had stopped, not a car had driven by to break our reverie. Not a sound. We drove at a walk. A small brick shrine graced the roadside to the left, with a pale marble Madonna and a candle. Snuffed. Past it was the ancient vineyard with the tree-sized vines, the rows about ten paces apart. In the old days there would be some wheat between some rows, corn between others, sunflowers between the next. The countryside was once as colorful as a Persian carpet. We passed another Madonna, glazed, colored terra-cotta, with a rusty grill to protect her. *"Palazzo Venturi"* said the sign. We turned in. Stone garden walls. Chapels. Open belfries with two pretty bells. A big yard between the outbuildings and not a soul around. Silence. And sun. A rook rasping, gloating in the trees. Then back out onto the road, and along a narrow ridge. At a small hamlet straddling the road, Mocine, we stop. There's a pretty stone well. A big long farmhouse, brick arches, rusty gates. A walled yard with great paving stones and a once-red oxcart faded pink, full of staves. In times past they used bull's blood for paint. I can't imagine what a ferocious red it must have been for a time. It is so pale and pink now. Pink like a child's toy. High on a wall, its glazing chipped, the family crest, buffalo horns over it, like protective angel wings, to keep the family from harm. And in the crest, pheasants, wild boar, and white birds that look like skinny, free-range chickens. The road is barely three steps wide, squeezed between the houses. Clay pots full of free-range geraniums sit on the low walls of a pigsty. We smile.

The road narrows, so that two cars could pass only with care and good intentions. After a wooded gully I turn the Matra hard to the left down a rutted, rocky road because down the hill, fronting shadowed woods, is a house that even my dreams wouldn't dare conjure. *"La Canonica,"* the wood sign says. We roll down and shut off the motor. La Canonica is a tiny architectural wonder. Its heart is a little ancient chapel built of pale-pink travertine. Added on to it are smaller brick buildings, mere rooms, clinging like children to their Mom. Around the chapel is a brick *piazzetta*, an old travertine bench and some trees for shade. A dream's dream. But we're too late. The windows and doors are all remade, and there are flowers in big vases along the wall, and iron garden chairs and a table under a tree, and a cup and saucer and an open journal. And down in the terraced garden, pruning sheers in hand, tall, cropped gray hair, and looking more content then any decent person has the right to be, a stiff-backed, proud-to-be-German German, glaring at us, beaming victory.

"Drive on, James," the voice of reason beside me says, and I start rolling and try to make a disdainful turn but, with the ignition off, the wheel is locked, and I hit the brake but that too hardly holds, and I almost push the *kleine arkitekturen vunderhoff* off into the bloody woods.

Back on the road is an old travertine pedestal with a tap. The water is fresh and cool and I wash my face and cool my neck and feel much less murderous for it. We drive on to a hamlet, Poggio alle Monache, and the sign, *"Monte Oliveto*, 2 km." It's well before noon. "Let's walk there," Candace says. And her eyes alight. I don't even counter. She has intuition that I have learned to trust. I put the Matra in the shade of a tree then we're off—the great explorers, great adventurers. But arm in arm. Following the signs.

This has become a tradition, leaving the car within walking distance of some ancient marvel that we're about to find. Better to sense the surrounding countryside—sounds, smells, the wind. And walking there, taking time, approaching the place the way it was meant to be—at an unhurried pace—might let us feel that sense of purest wonder that a traveler must have felt centuries ago, when sighting the end of a long and uncertain journey.

We passed a road that branched off to Chiusure, but we

headed south, descending. The hills were steeper here, drier, with sudden drops, gorges, sparser woods, then as we came over a rise, we were suddenly in a place that God must have abandoned on the third day of creation. There was the firmament and a bit of earth, but that earth was a towering eruption of barren clay cliffs, eroded into perpendicular, jagged, knife-blade ridges.

The road wound down into a dark cypress forest. A half-mile later—suddenly, unexpectedly—wedged so tightly in the forest that the boughs of the cypresses brushed against its walls, rose a medieval tower and an adjoining fortress wall. Below the wall across a now dry moat, lay a wooden drawbridge, its heavy, rusted chains vanishing in fissures in the walls. Pigeons cooed in niches under the balustrades, and among the cypresses a rook croaked a warning. Past the bridge and through a gloomy brick tunnel basked an autumn garden. There was no one anywhere. The old bridge groaned beneath our feet. Nestled under the archway of the entrance was the first sign that we were entering an abbey. It was an imposing Della Robbian terra-cotta scene glazed in blues and yellows. In its center, life-sized, sat an endearing, clear-eyed, country-girl Madonna, and in her lap, a cheerful baby Jesus swung a chubby leg. Above them hovered a pair of angels. We went in.

The herringbone brick floor of the tunnel was dank and uneven, but in the sunshine of the garden roses bloomed, and bougainvillea drooped, and jasmine crept on a trellis. There was the smell of roasting meats in the air. Past the garden, a narrow ridge led through steep woods but the abbey was nowhere. The silence made us whisper.

We took a round-worn, heaving brick path descending past a tiny chapel on a rise and a fenced-in flock of chickens on the left. A sonorous, melancholy sound rocked the air—the sound of great bells tolling just ahead. As if awakened from some lengthy slumber, the roosters behind us crowed. It was half past noon. We stood and listened. As our friend Sandro was to say later, there are only two sounds that suit the peaceful countryside: church-bells and roosters. A hawk circled near the sun, correcting its bank only now and then. There was still not a soul anywhere.

We went on. On our right, a spacious clearing broke, and under a long wall that held the hill, lay an abandoned brick *piazza*. Below it was an immense brick *vasca*, a basin, of pharaonic proportions, maybe fifty strides long, and twenty-five strides wide, and as deep as three grown men. It was only half full with greenish water now. Its size and the immense sound of the bells warned us that something imposing lay ahead. We turned off the path. The *piazza* was warm with sun. We heard footsteps. On the brick path a monk in white, his face hidden by his hood, shuffled with hurried care. There was a tiny chapel notched into the hill, its rosy plaster faded and peeling, its old wood doors cracked from the sun. About eye-height were cut two holes, to spy on those within or those without, and we pressed our faces against the warm wood to look in. A large peeling fresco of a most pious saint hung above the altar. A few benches. Old flowers. Age. We sat down on the stoop of the chapel, me against the wall, Candace against me, closed our eyes, and let the autumn sun soak down to our bones. Such silence. A dry autumn leaf brittled across the worn brick in the breeze. We sat.

The bells tolled one. It was time to eat.

Few things spark me to life like the prospect of a Tuscan lunch. We followed the path back to the odor of roasting meats, and sure enough on the *terrazzo* below the tower, in the sun-flecked shade of the jasmine-covered trellis, tables were set with white linen. We took one. My God, how well we ate. We were alone outside in that warm sunlight—a few locals wandered inside for lunch—and the two almost identical sisters who cooked and served brought us a continuously remarkable fare. There was homemade ravioli stuffed with ricotta and wild mushrooms, wild hare in a piquant sauce, roasted vegetables, and a red wine as robust as the clay. Then ricotta with wild berries. Then a great espresso and a long, slow *grappa* with our faces to the sun. It was almost three. We were ready for culture.

Past the *vasca*, at the bottom of the path, the stark brick mass of the abbey erupted against the cypresses and the wooded hills. To the left rose a squat building, to the right, an enormous square bell tower, topped by a turret in swirling patterns of scalloped brick that seemed from the *Arabian Nights*. But straight ahead stood the most striking part of all. Connecting the abbey to a massive tower, a three-story-high brick bridge stood, transparent with its many windows and delicate-pillared glassed-in arches above. And crossing the glass bridge in flowing white robe, strolling at a pace of gentle thought, was a hunched, ancient monk, back-lit by the sun.

Doors opened and shut; there was movement in the courtyard where the sign read, "*Camere degli ospiti.*" Rooms of guests. The front door of the abbey was unlocked with a grating sound. We went in. There was no one anywhere. Glowing in the half-light were the sensuously smooth and hollow-worn terra-cotta floors. This professedly most ascetic of places oozed sensuousness at every turn. Its languid woods, its walk, the great *vasca*, the see-through bridge, and now its leathery, undulating floors. After the gloom of the entryway we stepped out into the most sensuous place of all: *il chiostro*, the cloister. It was awash with the fragrance of gardenias.

A vaulted, covered walkway supported by arches surrounded the great quadrangle of the courtyard. Life-size frescos adorned the walls under each vault, and those perfect arches were enclosed by leaded glass, full of imperfections, that distorted the golden light. And my God what a courtyard. The brick pavement was strewn with terracotta vases, the bulbous kind that once held olive oil, the kind in which Ali Baba hid his forty thieves. The vases were filled with torrents of orchids, sage, gardenias, carnations and October Daphne. A plump, white-robed monk walked from vase to vase, pinching, watering.

The frescos by Signorelli and Sodoma were full of white-robed monks. They narrated the life of Saint Benedict, the founder of the order: his leaving school, leaving home, becoming a hermit, teaching, and performing a mixed handful of ho-hum and impressive miracles. Most of them are set in dreamy landscapes. And most of them are filled with unique, passionate faces and—even more remarkably—with curvaceous, sensuous, voluptuous figures. Inserted among the austere monks are coyly posed androgynous youths, with seductively bared limbs or hips askew in paint-tight tights; and women of soft, languid limbs and dreamy eyes and dresses so tumbling, so filmy, they seem to be mere folds of colored light. There are in Sodoma's "Evil women sent to the monastery," two such tantalizing, enticing women that I glance instinctively about to see if there might just still be one around; and Signorelli's coy, plump serving girl with her head innocently tilted and her skirt alluringly raised past her hip makes me stare in awe—they shouldn't allow so much wine at lunch lest the visitors drown in a sea of impure thoughts. And then I come to the scene of "Benedict tempted to impurity, overcomes temptation" and I move quickly on, lest my impure thoughts get overcome and ruin all my fun.

And beyond the naked columns, skin-smooth floors and loose-limbed arches, we pass the door of the monastery's cantina and inhale the fragrance of aging wine. I glance down corridors at the humble, bedded cells, the rooms for guests needing a retreat, where one might honor and cherish one's lawful wedded wife—awash in all this sensuousness who'd dare call that sin?

The bells toll and the walls tremble. It's five thirty. Closing time. We walk down the empty corridors, down the long stairs to court-yard level, where a reprimanding monk stands and stares right at us. We halt. But it's a fresco. We hurry past the courtyard, over the silken tiles, to the big wooden door where an ancient monk awaits us—live this time—with caving features and bare head and hands clasped behind him. He watches us. We mumble *buonasera* and step out onto the *piazza*. A pink-laced golden light has displaced the air. The walls are fiery above. A soft, three-quarter moon snuggles near the tower. The long, Tuscan twilight has begun.

We walk long-shadowed, arms around each other across the *piazza* and begin the shady climb. A blackbird's cry rings from the walls behind us. Across the gorge, the hills have lost all substance— diffused into layers of undulating light. Autumn leaves flame near the *vasca*. The sun lies in rare patches in the woods. A beaten earth trail leads up a tiny knoll. We go, climbing over steps of exposed roots with flickers of light to lead us. A broken travertine column, man height, stands alone in the woods, with a rusty cross imbedded in its top. With all the expanse of monumental architecture, all this art, this seems the only holy spot.

~

Out on the road a three-wheeled Ape comes chugging by. We wave it down and motion into its open back and Candace says, *"Un passaggio, per favore,"* and points to the top of the hill. The dusty bricklayer laughs and waves us aboard. The Ape chug-chugs feistily ahead. On the hilltop before a small cemetery we knock, get off and wave good-bye. We walk into the olive grove and sit in the dry grass on the bluff. The monastery and the whole world lie before us. Purples, yellows, pinks and blues but all washed, hazy, indefinite, dreamy. The world was dissolving, vanishing. And if you half-closed your eyes, you could see yourself from afar, dissolving in the haze. You could see yourself turning into light.

9 ~ HOME SWEET CASTLE

*O*n the fifth morning, while rekindling coals of the night before and putting slices of bread on a grate above them to toast, I kept seeing visions of courtyards full of voluptuous figures and flowers, tremulous light, and those silent hills. So much space, such silence, so much time. To drift. To think. To let your mind roam anywhere it pleases. To dream. Perhaps the true luxury of our age is not the piles of goods we endlessly accumulate, but Time. And perhaps the truest freedom is to be left alone. To gaze at the hills as long as you want. To go for a walk forever if you choose. And to have at every turn an inexhaustible natural beauty and centuries of man-made wonders. Maybe there lies the deep appeal of Tuscany.

Outside in the sun the cows were back, tethered farther down, scribing new circles in the dew-soaked hay. So content. And why not? They had their nice stone house in Tuscany. Over breakfast we decided to try a new approach to finding ours. We would move our search northward into the Chianti hills.

We drove into Rada Di Chianti where an Englishwoman had oh so much to sell. And there were indeed some spectacular places, but we arrived a few decades too late. The best old houses with the best locations had already been renovated mostly by foreigners. And the renovated places not only carried exorbitant price tags, but were often poorly and thoughtlessly restored. Garish new materials were mixed with the subtle old, or there were changes that tore the soul from a centuries-old house, and imposed on it some tawdriness the new owners brought nostalgically from home.

And the steep Chianti hills, much less soft and gentle than those near our cherished abbey, afforded only rarely the long, sea-of-hills vistas that we loved. Absent was that infinite, shimmering light that dissolves all matter before your eyes, and lets you drift in a kind of dream. So after three days and a dozen disappointments, we returned defeated to our falcon roost at Palazzuolo Alto.

And it rained. The clouds shrouded our entire mountaintop in a fog that stripped away the whole world and left us nothing but a few pine needles. I tried to remind myself of what Candace had said, about the gift of inward-turning the rain can bring, but no matter how hard I tried, all I could see was this poor sucker on a hilltop, houseless in Tuscany, staring at those dumb pine needles floating in the fog. The fog stayed two days. Candace painted happily below. I sat by the fire glaring at our hiking map, which had upon it the name of every old farmhouse in the Siennese hills. None of them mine. I read them all like one obsessed. At night, untired, I lay there with the names floating before me—Villanuova, Poderina, Montefresco, Bellavista—counting Tuscan farmhouses as others counted sheep, until the fog seeped in through the cracks of the windows and obliterated everything.

The third day of rain the phone rang. Our house is found. A friend of Joyce's had found us just the place, and he had a castle to boot, to which we were invited for lunch. The fog lifted. The pine needles settled back onto their branches.

A glorious morning! Winding straight north from Palazzuolo toward Florence, the road was empty, the air laced with autumn freshness. We talked about Paolo, a ceramist, the castle owner we were about to meet, who had bought a half-ruined, abandoned castle ten years before and restored it with the help of friends and traveling musicians. He provided concert space and lodging in exchange for hauling and chipping stones. That settled it. If some potter could rebuild an entire bloody castle, I sure as hell had the wherewithal to redo a bitty house. After all didn't I build myself a house-boat in my late teens, finish off an oceangoing sail-boat in my twenties? I had experience dammit. If Mr. Spin-the-mud could do a castle, hell I could do a whole medieval town!

We met Paolo in the piazza of a small town called Bucine. He was energetic, charming and witty *and* spoke English. We hit it off at once. With pulses pounding, we followed him up into the hills where the vines oozed their brightest colors that very day. We stopped in the middle of nowhere before a small, two-story struc-ture, which Paolo said was the guest house above and the *cantina* —the wine cellar—below. The arched *cantina* doors were open wide, and we were enveloped by the cool fragrance of wood barrels exhaling the bouquet of aging wines.

Huge casks lurked in the shadows of the cellar, and before us, perched upon a ladder, a studious-looking man our age was pumping wine from a spigot at the bottom of an enormous wood-en vat back into its top. He greeted us, mercifully in both Italian and English, then came down. Handshakes and introductions. He was the owner of the villa—which we were yet to see—a professor by profession and a wine maker by passion.

He explained to us that the pressed grapes fermenting in

there had to be "pumped over" twice a day to keep the temperature of the wine from climbing too high under the "cap," the floating mass of crushed grapes above the wine. Then there are the yeasts. Pumping over aerates the crushed grapes and the must, enabling the yeasts, the true makers of the wine, to multiply. It was my first lesson in winemaking. I was fascinated. But where was the house?

He led us up a shaded stairway, telling us how he came here ten years ago knowing nothing about wine except that he loved drinking it, and decided to make the best wine in Tuscany. He went against everything his neighbors knew. Planted tight rows instead of wide ones and used no fertilizer. His vines were pallid and the grapes tiny, and to the horror of his neighbors, he cut off and threw away clusters of grapes before maturation, "thinned," to send all the sugars and minerals into fewer grapes, better concentrating all the flavors. And when his neighbors tasted the grapes during harvest they were speechless. Not only were the grapes loaded with sugars guaranteeing strength, but they had complex flavors guaranteeing a sophisticated wine. But when can we see the house?

He asked if we cared to taste one of his 1985 vintages. I lightened up. I knew that '85 had been a spectacular year in France, so what the hell, the house could wait a couple of sips. We went down a narrow staircase into an underground brick vault. The walls were lined to the low ceiling with dusty bottles of wine. He searched a moment, uncorked, poured for himself, tasted, then poured for us. The color was a bountiful red-brown, with a brooding bouquet of exotic spices. We toasted, chin-chin, and we drank. His wine was supple, with a deep complexity that tingled all the taste buds. We passed compliments and sipped again. We chatted. Then my glass was empty. He offered just another bit and filled it.

We sipped. Then my brain got foggy. My tongue turned to cotton. "Sixteen degrees," I heard a voice say in the fog. "You can do it if you don't fertilize." I promised I wouldn't fertilize even if they tortured me. "I have fifteen thousand bottles" he went on, "and they all come with the house." "Damn the house!" cotton-tongue said. "Who needs a house? We'll live here. Get a stool and a bed and live right here. And maybe die here. But not before we make a swell dent in these bottles." There was polite laughter and a pinch in my ribs. A voice in the clouds said let's go see the house.

We went.

The house stunk.

My brain might have been foggy but my eyes were clear and they saw right away that the house stunk. Big time. It was a giant, dull, block-shaped thing straight from the Mussolini years. The interior spaces were perfect for speed-skating. They echoed. The place was as homey as a squash court. The roof leaked, streaking the walls, which at least gave the place some character. We asked some polite questions, paid polite compliments then went out and looked at the nonexistent view. But I kept thinking about all that wine below. Then some merciful angel mentioned lunch. We parted, and the owner generously presented us with a bottle of his finest. I felt so bad I almost blurted that I'd buy his multiplex.

~

We wound up a steep mountain road, and as we neared a tiny town, Paolo told us to study the people to see if we noticed something strange. It was near one o'clock and the streets were as full as a tiny town's can be, kids and young women and men everywhere. To me they looked perfectly normal. Then Candace, still looking back, said, "There are no old people."

"None," Paolo said.

I was shocked. If any single thing is typical of a small Italian town, then it's all the old people in it.

"S.S. retribution," he went on. "Ten for one. When the resistance blew up armored cars killing their officers, the S.S. killed everyone in town. Nobody you saw was born before the war."

Candace kept looking back. There was a long, deep silence. Only the motor whined, pushing all that metal up the hill.

We finished the trip in silence. Those hills had lost their warmth for me: all that horror in the soil, in the walls, in the trees.

"Home sweet home," Paolo said. And the evil was swept to the back of my mind. His castle was a dream.

Tiny. Perfect for a family. Around a small courtyard there was only one large structure, the modest-sized sunken concert hall. The rest were small, on a human scale. Inside, narrow staircases wound and vanished in darkness. The rooms were cozy. The walls, as much as five feet thick, felt alive; the stones were simply white-washed over to give light. The furniture was sparse, old and friend-ly; the place was truly a home. We could not stop our flood of sin-cere compliments but all the same I turned green with envy. And if his castle weren't enough, Paolo made wonderful, giant, abstract ceramic pieces, and a devilishly fine spaghetti sauce.

We had lunch in a small room in the tower with the win-dows open and the warm forest fragrance drifting in. Somewhere in another part of the castle, someone played an oboe, and its melody, amplified by the walls around the courtyard, drifted in the air. The afternoon meandered on. The wine hushed my restless-ness, and I relished the food, the castle, the excellent company, and only now and then did I look longingly through the window searching the hills below for my ruin in Tuscany.

10 ~ THE TUSCAN SEA

*T*hat night the phone rang. It was Giovanna, Candace's best friend
and our loft-mate during their art-school days in New York. She
was in Milan visiting her parents and she was coming tomorrow to
stay for a few days. Our meditative mountain solitude was over.
Giovanna is little and blond and cherub-pretty, and is alternately
irresistible and uproariously funny or self-absorbed and monu-
mentally dull. She designs high-priced shoes in New York and
paints wonderfully but her true passion is getting married. Often.
She had been married three times by the time she was twenty-
seven. Between marriages #2 and #3 she lived with us for a year on
Crosby street in Soho in a vast loft where we froze in the winter
and sweated on sweltering summer days. And in the sweltering
summer nights, to compensate for the lack of moving air, the two
ravishing, graceful women dressed scantily in roller skates and little else, circled slowly around the loft with bodies gleaming and
faces radiant. And below the open windows, the garbage-men
played war games with the garbage cans 'til dawn.

Giovanna was now twenty-nine, and she stepped into the

house, put down her bag, and announced with theatrical simplicity, "I'm moving back to Italy. I'm getting a divorce."

"Wipe your feet," Candace said.

"Aren't you even upset?" Giovanna asked, hurt.

"Not if you wipe your feet," Candace said. "Now give me
a hug and I'll get you some nice boar sausage to nibble before
dinner."

"Some friend! I'm getting a divorce and you offer me
nibbles."

"The last time you weren't getting a divorce was Christmas
four years ago, but only because you cooked all day and it somehow slipped your mind. Boar or no boar?"

"Boar."

"You took the word right out of my mouth," I said.

"That's it, gang up on me," Giovanna said and marched into
the fireplace and sat.

"Does this mean you're moving in with us?" I inquired like
a good host.

"Tell me what the house you bought is like first."

"We haven't found one yet."

"I told you that on the phone," Candace said, "but you
weren't paying attention because the sentence didn't contain your
name."

Giovanna turned to me and smiled. "And how is *your*
divorce coming along?" she asked.

We had a glass of wine and they cooked. They were always
best friends but even better when they cooked together. Giovanna
has that rare knack of cooking with whatever ingredients fall into
her hands, inventing as she goes, and coming up with things that
somehow taste classic.

"You have no herbs" she announced looking in the cupboards. "I'll have to go and find some."

It was dark outside. We had no flashlight so she rummaged through drawers, dug up a half-dozen candle stubs, attached them to a pot lid, lit them, and holding the lid at arm's length, went out into the darkness. Like a sorceress at some medieval rite, she kept along the ditch, stopping, gathering. She came back with her hand full of leaves and sprigs and desiccated stems. "Fennel for the rabbit stew," she announced, "and *malva*, *borragine* and rosemary for the pasta."

We ate, wedging the pot lid into a long crack in the mantelpiece to act as chandelier, and, lacking music, Giovanna provided melodious laments about her delusions: her third husband who after five years could not recall whether or not she took sugar in her coffee, about America where she refused to return to if they elect a man for president who has a voice that made fingernails on a blackboard sound like bird song. Then the phone rang and, convinced it was for her, she jumped to get it, and talked on and on, and only after a long time did we figure out it was Joyce, whom she had never even heard of but would probably have married if her dinner wasn't getting cold.

When she finally came back, she announced calmly, "Your Tuscan dream house is somewhere between Montepulciano and Montalcino. It's the most beautiful part of Tuscany and that is where we will look. The day after tomorrow. Because tomorrow I will take you to see my favorite sea." And she sat down and sighed, "I'm glad I'm here to take care of you." Then, for no apparent reason, she broke into a perfect two-part Yogi Bear and Bubu imitation, *in Italian,* all the more hilarious for being unintelligible, and she went mercilessly on until we had pains behind our ears from laughing. Then we went outside and watched a huge moon rising through the branches.

~

I was awakened by an ornery cow somewhere down the road. It was dawn. I went down to the kitchen to make coffee. The house was silent. I sat and looked out at the world unfurling from the darkness.

We breakfasted, talking softly, still mellowed by deep sleep. Then we packed bathing suits and towels—just in case the summer heat lingered in the sea—repacked the cheese and wine, and left before we saw the sun. As we drove by the cemetery, only the tips of the cypresses glowed golden.

At Siena we veered south. The hills were mercilessly dry and empty here, then further south they steepened and there were only woods. A hazy air tumbled through the valleys from the west. Giovanna pulled down the window, took a deep breath and announced, "I smell iodine. We're near the sea." We had been gone less than an hour. This miracle of sudden change is one of the never-ending joys of Tuscany. It's hard to believe that one can leave after breakfast, by car or train, and arrive in plenty of time for lunch in Venice, Naples, Portofino, or Rome.

And then there is the sea. One seldom thinks of the sea when one thinks of Tuscany, conjuring instead its inland sea of hills, forgetting the long coast on the Tyrrhenian, with vast unin-habited stretches, dark pine forests, cliffs, and the medieval harbors of sailboats and fishing boats with their bows anchored to sea. The tiny houses, shoulder to shoulder on the hills and bluffs, gaze down at the transparent water whose hues shift with the rising and fad-ing light.

We headed south on the Aurellia, the old Roman road running parallel to the sea but one tall ridge of wooded hills removed. That ridge is the long nature reserve of Monti dell'Ucellina, with only footpaths to penetrate it, giving the seabirds and the wind that desolate, sheer coastline to themselves. At its southern tip, a spur of high-bluff land juts out to sea, crowned by the fortressed town of Talamone—an Etruscan city three thousand years ago—its castle against the sky protecting its minute harbor below.

It was still early morning and we walked along the harbor, where four fishermen were hauling a skiff, ample-sterned and double-ended, onto the stony shore. Using tree limbs as rollers and a First World War jeep that gasped and sputtered after every lurch, one fisherman stood in the stern so his weight would raise the bow, one cursed and flailed the jeep, another moved the rollers, and the fourth, with his pants rolled up to his knees and his hands planted on his hips, stood picturesquely in the water for no imaginable reason other than he saw the pose in a film long ago.

We penetrated the massive town walls, up a narrow shady stairway, past tables and folded umbrellas of a still closed *trattoria*, and climbed up and up into the empty *piazza* where an old priest, shored up by a much-older lady, toddled, shuffling loudly, across the sun-drenched stones. A narrow street angled upward, and from its shade, we burst onto the bluff. The waveless, clear blue sea stretched into the distant mist which hid islands of charmed names: Corsica, Sardegna, Elba and Monte Cristo. The lazy sea lapped at the crooked rocks below. Gulls shrieked.

"My God, this is beautiful," Candace said.

"Let's sail somewhere," I said.

"We just got here," Candace said.

"My life's in tatters," Giovanna said.

"Don't jump. You'll spoil lunch," Candace said, taking her by the arm, and they walked toward the north edge of the bluff beyond which the forested hills of the Ucellina towered. Behind us stood the fortress, and across the bay, a small hotel and its hanging gardens clung to the cliff, above the handful of hostile rocks it called its beach. On a small stone platform were a handful of blue beach umbrellas and lounges, but only a single bather ankle-deep in sea.

Back on the Aurellia, we headed south toward L'Argentario, a rugged cone-shaped mountain rising from the sea. It is joined to the mainland by two long tongues of sand that create between them a salt-water lagoon where gulls sweep and herons glide and egrets stand white and stiff against the green of the shore. The jagged coast is dotted with small villas, eucalyptus, pines and the odd palm, and on tiny, desperate terraces a few olives and sprigs of vine. On the roof of a restaurant below the road, a chunky lady leaned a coarse sign against the chimney, "*Oggi, zuppa di pesce.*" Fish soup today. Just ahead was the old Spanish fort-town of Porto Santo Stefano.

It's an honest, unquaint town, the quay strewn with fishnets, mounds of fishnets, reefs of fishnets, and bales of fishnets carefully folded and covered with old rugs and tightly roped like packs of a caravan preparing for a journey. More nets were stretched out across the quay, being mended by fishermen whose hands are as gnarled and knobby as their coastline. Rows of awninged fish-stands are cut into the hill along the shore, with their striped curtains hanging low to keep the sun off the gleaming fish laid out in long trays. There are endless shapes and colors of fish and mollusks, like a still and too-well-ordered aquarium. There are exotic, square-headed, pink *gallinella*; silvering small tuna looking bullet-fast even in death; great flat white-bellied toad-tails; tiger-striped and fluorescent *sgombri*; brown *murena* eels that some still catch at night by lantern light; giant eyed *friturrina* for frying quickly in olive oil; red-eyed, red-gilled *alici*; and the sad-faced *dentice*. Beside them ooze masses of octopus and squid, and *orate* and *merluzzo*, *spigole* and *rombi*, and *bianchetti* as tiny as the white of our finger-nails and sold by the wooden ladle-full, and sea snails and *luma-chine* and *scugili*, the pointed spike shells that kids love to collect, and the fishwife yelling, *"Chi servo?"*

The sound of a hammer hitting heavy iron rang out as three fishermen grappled to lay an eye-splice in steel cable. They hammered the wire apart, fed the tail through three times, cursed and hammered, then rammed a huge marlinspike through it. One of them held, and another twisted and the third furiously uncurled the tail to lay the braid. The one twisting shouted, *"Giri! Giri! Giri!"* and the uncurler rebutted, *"Giro, giro, giro, Madonna Affogata"*—I'm turning, I'm turning, for the Drowned Madonna!

Their accents were like those of Napoli, and the names of the fish boats, *Santa Maria, Santa Lucia, Angelo Padre, Salvatore*, all these holy names in antipapal Tuscany seemed out of place. I asked Giovanna if she would mind finding out a bit of history. Of course she went.

A solid, firm-limbed fisherman with short, curly gray hair and the clearest of blue eyes was greasing his shackles, and smiled broadly as she neared. They chatted for a while, his bright face explaining, his big greased hands describing details in the air. Then she came back and I could see in her eyes that the trip was worth-while. It seems that until after the Second World War, Porto Santo

Stefano was a sleepy fishing village, with but a few skiffs that fished the local waters and fed the local folk. The town lived on that and some farming, and some ferrying of goods to the small islands around. After the war, toward the fifties, the boats of the south began to frequent the waters, boats from Amalfi, and Napoli and Sicilia. They came for a few months and stayed many years, and their families came north and their friends came north, and Porto Santo Stefano now rings with the melodious voices of the Napoli and Amalfi and Sicilia and the boisterous camaraderie of the south fills the air.

We walked the waterfront at Porto Santo Stefano, among fishing boats with talismans on their masts: a great buffalo horn, a husk of corn, a small goat-horn—anything, to bring them back safely from the sea; among the floating voices, among skiffs being cleaned and cats searching for fish bits, down to the boatyard where a big wooden ketch was laid up on the ways. A man with his sleeves rolled was repainting the bottom, and a woman painted the boot-stripe right above. And in small black letters, the home port said New Zealand. And my heart yearned for the sea.

We forgot for a while the hills of Tuscany, and talked instead of living on the Tuscan sea, that is not some wide open emptiness like the oceans we have known, but a warm, blue unmarked seaway to Capri or Sicilia or Malta, or Tunisia just below, or to the east, the place of myths where it is said once you go you never come back again, where the islands are called Mykonos and Soros and Ikaria.

"The Tragedy of Choice, somebody wrote," Candace said.

"We need more lives," I said.

"And fewer husbands," Giovanna said.

"And lunch. I'm starving," Candace said.

"And wine. I'm thinking," Giovanna said, and she stepped around the fishnets, shooed away a harbor cat, and went to ask a fisherman sitting on a small stool that most urgent of questions, "Where does one eat best here without going broke?" The question seemed to be taking a long time even for her, and Candace, who has to eat when she has to eat or her Irish ire rises toward the homicidal, was getting antsy. "What can she be asking him?" she blurted.

"His hand in marriage," I said.

Giovanna came back with her face aglow. "I found paradise!" she said. "They make their own *fettuccini* and *pici* by hand, and they make *fettuccini alla seppia nera* and . . . " and she grabbed us by the arms and led us around the mounds of nets reciting in a feverish voice the menu. And the fishermen looked up from their nets and skiffs and one said approvingly, *"Fatto bene, Occhialino,"* and beamed. I asked Giovanna to translate, and she said flatly, "Well done, Four-eyes."

The thing I lust for more than Tuscan food is Tuscan seafood. It is cooked simply with olive oil, salt and black pepper, sometimes parsley and garlic, perhaps a splash of wine, and rarely—on the heavier-flavored sardines or tuna—with capers or tomatoes or olives. My god, I'm like Pavlov's dog just thinking about them all.

So we rushed like three obsessed back to the Matra, and we wound through town, through the mob of kids pouring out of school running, weaving, dodging, chasing and stopping and gaping at the weird little car with three people in three bucket seats side by side by side. Then we were out in the countryside, still climbing, and heading farther and farther out to sea. The lush *macchia mediterranea,* the low, dense, broad-leafed evergreen forest thickened dense around us. Giovanna described every plant. There was *corbezzola* with its glistening leathery leaves and glowing red fruit the size of cherries but with a rough stubbly skin that titillates your tongue. And *lentaggine,* which grows slowly hence its name, and the regal *leccio,* the ilex, whose leaves resemble that of the olive but its fruit is like a graceful acorn. The country was steep and rough and untilled, desperately terraced only now and then. To our right the precipice fell into the mesmerizingly blue sea, the sun now high, the sea glare gone, the blue darkening in the depths.

My God I was famished.

The *trattoria* was sculpted into the face of the bluff below the road. It teetered over the crag. Below it, gorges fell lushly to the sea. A footpath meandered to a group of houses carved into the landscape, their walls made of the same stone as the crags, their roofs of thick verdant sod as green as the pasture at our feet. And where the sea lapped the rocks far below was a twisted, rocky island, swept by gulls, with a fishing skiff laying out nets in the lee.

In the late of October we were alone. The *padrone* and his family were eating at a table near the kitchen and we wished them *"Buon appetito,"* and Giovanna said, as if it were a ticket of admission, "Andrea sent me," and said the fish boat's name. This seemed to carry weight, for everyone wiped their mouths and the *padrone* extended a hand, said *"Benvenuti"* and ushered us around the corner to a table that seemed suspended in air below a palm. We sat gingerly. They poured us a glass of a fine Banfi *spumanti,* and unsolicited—perhaps seeing the hunger in our eyes— brought us a plate of magnificently varied warm seafood bites. Perhaps they always cooked this well, or perhaps Andrea was not to be let down, but the dishes that followed were certainly among the most unaffected we had eaten, fresh and unpretentious, but full of all the natural flavors of the sea.

We followed the warm antipasto with an *insalata di mare Toscana*, a cold seafood salad with a splendid mixture of clams, mussels, squid, warm octopus slices, and some large shrimp fresh from the shell, all steamed then bathed in olive oil and freshly squeezed lemon juice, with black olives, sliced garlic, thinly diced yellow and red peppers, and fresh chopped parsley. I honestly don't recall when I had tasted more varied delicate flavors in one bite. And they brought us a dry white wine from Elba. We begged for time to catch our breaths, and had some wine, gazed out to sea and ordered pasta. Candace and I had our beloved *spaghetti alle vongole*, and Giovanna *fettuccini alla seppia nera,* black pasta with cuttlefish that made her tongue and her teeth and her lips as black as night. "Black like my heart," she said.

"Shut up, Johnny, and eat your goop like a good boy," Candace said.

Then they brought us a big grilled *dentice,* his pensive forehead furrowed with thought, and *verdura alla griglia* and a small *porcino* gently grilled and bathed in olive oil. Then we went out on the terrace that the sun had heated through, for espressos and *grappa*. My God life is grand. The afternoon breeze had risen and the brilliant sun now danced on the sea. The fisherman hauled in his nets, and, anchorless, let the sea breeze push him back toward the harbor. In the long, curved wavelets that flowed from the tips of the island, the gulls bobbed.

The owner chatted with Giovanna, accompanied us outside and waved good-bye. "He told me about a secret cove where some Spanish general's wife escaped with her lover some century or other," Giovanna said. We followed a steep footpath forever down. Then we broke into a tiny cove, a crevice really between two looming outcroppings. The beach was sea-smoothed rock. The tide was out. The rocks warm. We found a gentle hollow and sat with our backs against the sun-warmed bluff, eyes closed. We sat in blissful silence. "You know," Giovanna finally began, "I know I should be distraught, but I haven't felt so . . ."

"Oh please do shut up!" Candace said.

11 ~ HAND ME A BRICK

*W*e slept like the dead, but rose driven by house-hunting fever. As the sun climbed over the hill we were already descending into the fog of the valley. We had decided to start from Montepulciano and work our way west through Pienza on to Montalcino. The Michelin marked that entire road green, meaning the countryside around it is of remarkable beauty. If we found nothing there I was for moving to Sarasota and taking up lawn bowling. We had but two weeks left.

The fog thickened. Tractors, Apes, and Cinquecentos burst from the fog then vanished again. After Torrita I felt the road beneath us start to climb and the fog thinned, and the pale sun hovered pink. Then we were above the fog and the hilltops bobbed before us like islands in a sea. Towering over them, its ramparts, steeples and domes aglow in the morning sun, Montepulciano floated in the shimmering light.

The countryside was the most beautiful we had seen, the hills as soft and welcoming as those leading to the abbey, but even more verdant. We left the car beside a park where three old men played bocce below the fortress wall, and on a backless stone bench a girl sat astride her boyfriend's lap, planting everlasting kisses on his lips, oblivious to us, the old men, the world. Life was for kissing.

We walked up the hill, toward the forbidding walls of the town. Behind us was the striped travertine facade of the four-teenth-century church of Sant'Agnese, and ahead of us the curving, narrow street lined with masterfully carved door frames and great windows. Embedded in the facade of one *palazzo* were Etruscan bas reliefs, plaques, and an urn.

Narrower alleys, *vicoli*, some vaulted with more structures rising above the vaulting, twisted away into the light above or the tufts of fog below. We climbed. My heart pounded. Another church with worn, irregular steps but a marvelous Renaissance travertine facade blocked the sky to our right. We went in. The church was empty. Life-size statues of a dead, reclining Christ lay peacefully in a niche. Enormous thorns. Great beads of blood. And just past him was a Madonna in blue, her breast full of daggers the size of kitchen knives, to show her pain.

Back in the street the fog was rising. People shuffled out of it, then into it and away. The street was lined with tiny shops: a greengrocer, a barber, a butcher, a store of small appliances, a shoe store, a button-and-thread store. Only the tiny shop of the cobbler teemed with life. The cobbler sat at his shoe-shaped anvil next to an enormous pile of shoes, and four men sat along the walls in fervent discussion. The cobbler's social club. Giovanna asked passers-by about an *immobiliare*, a realtor. People shrugged and apologized but they couldn't help. We went on.

In a small room at street level, an old man was weaving split twigs into a mantle around a demijohn. Out of big wooden *canti-*

na doors poured the cool fragrance of wine. Inside, the rows of barrels in the gloom was endless. The *cantinas* were dug at enormous depth into the hill. Giovanna inquired and was told that the entire town was honeycombed below with interconnected tunneling, secret passageways, storage caverns, escape routes, tombs, underground wells, bottomless traps. Then her face lit up: a *geometra*— a sort of builder-designer—might know of some old houses for sale. We almost ran to find his office, buzzed but there was no reply. Someone came out from the smoke-filled bar where men were playing cards, and said Geometra Lenni was not in today, but gave us his number. We smelled victory.

We climbed. The long, winding main street, Il Corso, ended in a vast *piazza* on the hilltop. Magnificent *palazzi*, a corner arcade and a most romantically carved well with a griffin and a lion atop it framed two sides of the square. A travertine-faced castle with a crenellated tower rose high above the north side, and on the west, atop broad steps, was the very best of all, Il Duomo. The cathedral from the sixteenth century. Its facade was stupendous. Unique. Unforgettable. There *was* no facade. Just a roughed-in front of bricks, notched, holed, jutting, thrown up with little care, awaiting the glorious facade of mosaic or marble that hadn't—just yet— arrived. Five centuries. . . . Why rush? . . . I *love* Tuscany.

A little kid with hair falling in his eyes was blasting a rubber ball with ferocious might against the wall under an arcade, and it resounded like a cannonade around the square. We searched between the buildings hoping to catch a view of the countryside below, but there were twists and turns and we found none. Giovanna, frustrated at our lack of success, turned on the kid and

yelled in her full voice, *"Ora basta, per la Madonna! Tu mi fa sorda!"*
Now enough. You're making me deaf! The kid stopped, turned to
Giovanna and I readied myself for some stinging, snide remark.
But he stared with big friendly eyes and said almost humbly, *"Mi
scusi Signora. Uno si dimentica."* Sorry, Lady. One forgets. Then
Giovanna gently asked him from where we could best see the valley bellow. His face lit up. *"La,"* he said, and pointed at the tower
that rose straight above us to the sky. *"Venite!"* he said. And ran. We
followed.

The tower's castle was the town hall, mostly empty, piles of
documents in one room, old chairs in another, and the *vigile
urbano*—the town's policeman—in his office, buried in the pink
newspaper *Tutto Sport*. We went up a wide, worn, stone stairway
then another and another, and the kid signaled for us to be quiet.
He swung open a small door with a hand-scribbled sign, *"Pericolo
di crollo."* We went in and shut the door. We were in the dark.
From somewhere far above, shreds of light revealed the rubble at
our feet, and a violently steep, narrow wooden staircase. The stairs
creaked and dust fell. *"Venite,"* the kid whispered from the gloom
above. We followed. The stairs groaned in concert under us. We
felt our way ever upward, but it got no lighter. We stopped to rest.

"What did the sign on the door say?" I whispered.

"Danger of collapse," Giovanna said.

"Mother of Christ!" I hissed. "We're going to die."

We crept. The stairs moaned incessantly. I tried stepping as
lightly as a fly. Then we heard pigeons. The light grew. Pigeon shit
carpeted the steps. "Paradise," Candace said.

"Could be," Giovanna said. "We're certainly high enough."
Then the pigeons above panicked and whipped the air, and dust
and feathers came down like gentle rain.

"Che bella!" Giovanna cried.

We were out. On top of the world. We were on the highest point for twenty miles around. The Apennines rose in the east, the old volcano in the west, and right below us, like some place lost in time, was a magical valley of small hills quilted with vineyards, olives, fields, ponds and a dusty ridge road that wound, like in a child's drawing, past a few old houses and their cypresses. Past the last lived-in house it fell into the valley, skirting ruins, a mill, a tower, across a glimmering creek, then rising and twisting upward to a tiny hill town a few miles away.

"I'm moving here," Giovanna said.

"Over my dead body," Candace said. "This valley is mine."

"By what right?" Giovanna complained.

"That you're at the parapet and I'm right behind you."

That settled that.

"Signora, posso?" the kid said. Lady, may I?

He was leaning over the parapet into the *piazza*, his ball raised and a careful smile spreading on his face. We looked down. The *piazza* seemed in another world far below, the *vigile urbano* in his white cap, his pink paper stuck under his arm, made his way slowly toward the newspaper kiosk. The kid looked pleading at Giovanna. And she, like an empress whose slightest signal could unleash armies, nodded her head. *"Buttalo,"* she said. Throw it.

The kid beamed. Then he threw. He threw the rubber ball with all his might, and it sailed out into the gleaming sky, arched past the swooping pigeons, out toward the patient brick facade, and then it fell, accelerating like a hawk in deadfall. "We're going to jail," I said. Then it hit—as loud as thunder—right beside the drowsy *vigile,* who in a remarkable feat leapt straight into the air and threw his arms above his head as if he meant to fly. The pink paper scattered. He roared, looked straight at us, and roared, *"Angelo, tu maledetto strullo, vagabondo imbecille, se io ti chiappo,"* but Angelo had ducked behind the wall. The *vigile* carried on in a miraculous performance that somehow bypassed the human need for air until Giovanna leaned over the parapet, waved and beamed a huge smile straight down. When the *vigile* finally paused she yelled, *"Mi scusi, Brigadiere, mi è scivolata dalle mani."* Excuse me Brigadier, it slipped out of my hands.

The *vigile* stared murderously, considered his few options, then raised his cap, and chided, *"Un po' d'attenzione, Signora. Mi raccomando!"* Then turned on his heel, and headed toward the bar across the way.

"You're a good Joe, Gio," Candace said. "You can live in my valley if you want."

The *vigile* froze in his steps, turned, and yelled a gleeful afterthought at us: *"Le scale crollano sotto di voi!"*

"What did he say?" we urged Giovanna.

"That the stairs will collapse under us," she said. "Hand me a brick."

The fog had gone. The sun blazed down out of a deep blue sky. The many-hued, clay-tiled roofs of town undulated at our feet. Nothing was quite square, and not a shape was repeated. The rows of houses, cheek by jowl on the curving streets, never quite shared a roofline: always a jut here a rise there. Wherever an open space remained, a tree or a vine or a vegetable garden flourished. Ramparts, churches and steeples everywhere. Within the walls of this town of two thousand souls, we counted seven domes or steeples. But the most magnificent of all, that of San Biagio, designed by Sangallo, lay outside the walls.

It was a structure with perfect rhythm, as simple as if built from old toy building blocks: cubes, arches, rectangles, triangles, a big cylinder and a dome. It was entirely of travertine aged to a sensuous glow, like some jewel in a field of green. The plan was a stubby, equal-limbed cross, the dome rising from its center, and the *campanile* set off from it slightly, freestanding, as high as the dome and needle-graceful. Sangallo had planned four spires, one in each crook of the cross, until maybe his Mamma told him, *"Piano, con calma.* You're building a church not a birthday-cake," and he let a good thing be.

I gazed back at that snaking dirt road, its ponds, its little homesteads in the pristine emptiness so close to this town. And my gaze fell on a house straight from my dreams. It was the very last lived-in house on the road, small, unpretentious, all alone on that ridge in the middle of the valley, surrounded by cypresses and an oval ring of thickets, with a vineyard on one side, and a pond just above. But some guy with pruning shears must have gotten to it first. It seemed in perfect shape, the land around it ordered. I forced my eyes away.

We drove west on a narrow road that was built with a single dictate: eliminate the straight. Michelin had marked it with good reason, for it wound through the dreamiest part of the hills of Tuscany: long views, short views, ruins, a castle and the old volcano. Pienza was a tiny jewel. It was smaller and more jovial than Montepulciano, lacking perhaps that mystery that one would like to have in the course of daily life. But there was a cozy, people-filled *piazza,* with its *duomo,* a town hall with its inviting *loggia,* the

Palazzo Piccolomini with its cool, tall courtyard and a magical hanging garden, and the old volcano beyond the town walls. Maybe we could live *inside* such a town. Maybe we could find a fine old *palazzo* with a tiny walled garden, a well, some flowers, and a table outside under a tree, near the little shops, the cafes, the bars, the cool churches in hot summers, the friendly *piazza* for a stroll in the mild evenings, chatting with friends. It seemed like a fine alternative to a place in the countryside. Until we drove back in the countryside.

We found the local *geometra*, and inquired if anything was for sale around Pienza, but there was nothing. The bells tolled eleven. It was time to prepare for lunch. We loaded up in the shops for a picnic, then drove into the country to find a place to eat.

"Turn here," Candace says at a barely standing farmhouse at a crossroads. The sign, small, bent and rusty, says "Sant' Anna in Camprena, 5km." The guide book says monastery from the fourteenth century. Abandoned. Many years later *The English Patient* would be filmed there.

The trees close in. The road dives and heaves and twists in shadows. Ruins everywhere. A medieval tower set strangely in a hollow; an small abandoned monastery, farmhouses, dark woods. Dirt roads vanishing in the undergrowth. A rutted road turns uphill to Sant' Anna. Enormous cypresses on guard on either side. At the top of the road, in the middle of nowhere, the high walls of the monastery church touch the road. On the other side, a short wall, and beyond it, past the boughs of an olive grove, the whole wide peaceful world rolling, empty and gentle to the west. We stop under the cypresses. Not a soul. Not a sound. A wing of the monastery huddles below. No signs of recent life. Around the back, with its wrought iron gate locked by a rusty chain, is a magnificent walled garden with a circular lily pond into which tall grasses and wild flowers droop. All around us, in the distance, church bells toll. But not here, where the great bells hang silent in the steeple. It's noon.

We take our picnic basket and a blanket and step over the short wall to a rise in the orchard where we can get a view of the whole world. Ancient gnarled olives. How can they live with the bark gone, the trunks twisted, hollowed? The olive grove is thick with wild grasses. We lay the blanket down under an olive, half in the shade for Candace, half in the sun for Giovanna. We unpack and uncork the wine. We lay the meats and cheeses, olives and tomatoes out on plates, the bread, a broad ring called *ciambella*, we break by hand. The wine goes in little stemless glasses and glows a brilliant chestnut-red in the sun. The sunlight trembles over us. We toast to more days like today. We eat. Then we toast to the One and Only Holy Roman Catholic Church for thoughtfully appropriating the most beautiful spots in Tuscany, and abandoning them to us. Then we just toast, period. How that wine glows in the light. Then we eat the *mille foglie*, a custard with thin pastry covered with icing sugar, and Giovanna toasts to Yogi and Bubu in Italian and we snort with laughter and have icing sugar mustaches all over our faces. We toast to the icing sugar.

The air trembles with the shrill of a cicada who must have mistaken a shadow for the night.

It's now mid-afternoon in the soft hills as we approach Montalcino. An improbable cluster of cypresses, maybe thirty, stand stark against the expanse of plowed hills. And a few cypresses, single or in pairs, dot the hilltops against the sky.

There's a twelfth-century fortress guarding the town's entrance, but above it rises a hill from which you could happily lob cannon balls at the town all day. It's a quiet town with steep staired *vicoli*, and an astounding number of gardens and green spaces within its walls, but it can't hold a candle to Montepulciano and the lost valley below it. Since we have been guzzling the Brunello made locally, we buy some more. As if by miracle, the owner of the *enoteca*, wine shop, dabbles in real estate, he shows us photos of two places, one near the main road the other in a gulch. We decline.

But there is a splendid little century-old cafe in the *piazza* under a huge tower, with tables under umbrellas and a giant *loggia* across the way, so we sit and have *spremuta*, orange juice squeezed fresh on the spot. The *piazza* slowly fills with early evening walkers. The cafe fills. The shadows lie long on the paving stones. Kids with backpacks come up the hill from school kicking a crumpled paper cup for a ball. And yell "*A me! A me!*"

We drive home through to the sunset. *Ti ammazzo* is sitting on her stairway silently feeding her doll with a spoon. We have a quiet dinner. Giovanna is leaving in the morning.

"You'll miss me," Giovanna says.

"Let's blow up some chestnuts," Candace says.

We drive her to the train through the early morning fog. It feels colder than it is. The little station has a few men in wool coats and silk scarves going to Florence and some train men. While we wait, Giovanna phones the *geometra* in Montepulciano, but it's too early, there's no reply. The train is late. It has only three old cars with their lights on. Hugs. Giovanna finds a seat and pulls down the window and the train begins to move. She leans out. Then something worrying comes to her mind.

"Hey next week's your birthday, Pal," she yells to me. "Where will you be?"

"In the poorhouse," Candace yells.

Giovanna laughs. The wind blows her blond hair across her face and she and the train vanish in the mist.

12 ~ LA MARINAIA

*W*e rush back to the house, and I wait by the phone, gathering up courage to make my first phone call in Italian, because if there is anything more terrifying than speaking a language you don't know, it's speaking that language on the telephone. And worse still is speaking that language on a telephone which has the clarity of sound of the shoe-polish cans connected by copper wire that we used as kids. Crackle, sizzle, hiss. *"Pronto, Pronto,"* says a voice from the grave. I do my memorized house spiel. He responds. I'm lost. I ask him if, through the infinite mercy of the Madonna, he speaks English. *"Niente."* French? *"Nulla."* Hungarian? He laughs. But he says—I think—that he understands French if I speak slowly. I respond, in French, that I might understand his Italian if he speaks slowly, and if he stops crackling, sizzling and hissing. He laughs.

It's working!

His voice is young, easy-going and he loves to laugh; already a good sign. So we chat a bit, I in French he in Italian. And I tell him what I'm looking for and he says slowly, *"C'è qualcosa,"* There is something. When can you come? He barely finishes his sentence and the Matra's motor is roaring and the tires spit gravel as I spin onto the road. Candace, having lost three full days of painting, stays home.

The fog's gone. The Matra flies. It takes the curves flat, and halfway in the curve you push your foot down and come out heart pounding and brace yourself for the next one. I no longer give a damn about the winding road dictating a slow pace; I have a home to find. In a halfhour I catch a glimpse of Montepulciano ahead in the clouds. As I dive into the last valley, it begins to rain and the Matra drifts through the curves but grips again. The town has vanished in the low clouds. I start up the last hill.

The park is empty. No lovers clutching in the rain and no *bocce*. I had forgotten the umbrella, so I pull tight the old waxed-coat and hat I bought in County Cork one August years ago. There too I had found an old tower to buy, but got frightened off when Candace and I, hurrying through drizzle, encountered a farmer slowly pushing a wheel-barrow and greeting us with, "Is it not a beautiful morning?" I cherished his spirit but loathed his weather.

The streets are deserted. Only a little shapeless gnome with a sour face stands at the door of his empty wine store. The mist sweeps down the streets. Geometra Lenni's office is on the second floor of an old *palazzo*. He's big and young, Marco Lenni, big handshake, big smile. We sit and chat and soon feel comfortable with the tandem language, each of us asking only now and then for clarification.

I recount to him the houses I have seen, what faults they had, not to criticize but to inform him of what we are looking for: a Tuscany as pristine as possible. And no sloppy renovation that I would first have to pay for, then tear down and do over. He agrees.

Then he tells me he has something, redone with perfect care, perfect taste, perfect originality. All alone. Spectacular silence, spectacular views. I beg to see a photo, a drawing, anything. He has nothing. Another listing by hearsay. But why don't we just drive and see it, he suggests. I jump out of the chair.

We walk out of town and drive under the ramparts and back up the hill, but it's impossible to say in the mist where we are. If there were a break in the cloud he could show me the house in the middle of the valley. My heart pounds. I don't dare think the thought, that just perhaps this house could be the one that I . . . Never mind. We get out. The mist is so thick we barely see the rooftops. But I sense something familiar and my heart pounds harder.

"Una vista splendida," Marco says and laughs his unaffected laughter.

Then we descend through the clouds. They thin as we drop. We pass walled gardens and the ramparts of a cemetery and turn onto a small road. *"Mon Dieu!"* I exclaim. Because a long cypress avenue stretches in the mist before us—one tree planted in honor of each local man who fell in the first big war—and at its end, almost glowing in its frame of towering cypresses, is the temple of San Biagio with its dome and *campanile* and those walls the color of sensuous flesh.

We turn into the countryside. The ramparts and the town are in the mist above. A mile or so farther and we turn again onto a dirt road that falls into the valley. I sense a familiarity and fall silent. I recognize the first homestead on the right but don't dare think it, just in case I jinx us. We drive. More familiar homesteads. Then the pond. I break out in sweat. At the vineyard I have to open the car window. Marco slows.

"*Ce n'est pas vrai,*" I gasp.

He turns down a tiny road, the house's own drive, with grass growing between the wheel ruts. It's all there: the cypresses, the well-tended garden, the oval ring of thickets all around. And the house. My god the house. About a hundred yards before us the house is huddled below its trees, the little house that I dreamed on from the ramparts the day before. It is beautifully restored with an inviting handmade-brick *piazzetta* before it, and a trellis with a table under it, and masses of grapevine over it, so bright and golden even in the mist. We go down a narrow stairway cut into the hill. Shrouding over us are *corbezzola* with fleshy green leaves and glowing-red berries, and pomegranate bushes with their improbable fruit like Christmas ornaments. And bushes of wild roses, rosemary, lavender, tall laurel and short thyme. And in big terra-cotta pots, fleshy plants with yellow flowers and geraniums still in bloom. And at the garden's end a huge poplar with yellow trembling leaves, and across from it an ancient oak with an enormous canopy.

Around us are only fields and vineyards and a flock of sheep on the hillside across the way. And silence—my God what silence—and even with the low clouds you can see the hills that roll on forever with only the odd ruin between us and the horizon. And I am babbling at Marco, I'm not sure in what language, about what a dream the place is, when the clouds part above, slowly, *piano piano*, with a bright glow around their edges. And in the great hole in the clouds, lit golden by the hidden sun are the ramparts, churches, houses and the towers—floating in the clouds like some Kingdom of Heaven—of the most beautiful hill town in Tuscany. I sit down.

"I'm home," I mumble. "They'll have to carry me from here feet first."

It might have been in Hungarian.

Marco doesn't have the keys, but goes to the farmhouse back up the road, where the lady who is looking after the house lives. I feel blessed. I can walk around alone and ogle in peace.

The house lies in the side of the hill, below an olive grove and a wheat field freshly plowed, edged by a row of cypresses, then a tall stone wall about a hundred feet in length. Next to the wall, roses and a wide, mossy-bricked walkway to the house. Below the house, hayfields drop down to a stream, whose winding banks are lined with poplars and big oaks and brambles where birds sing. The wind sweeps the clouds apart and with that sudden change of light that comes in Tuscany, the sky turns blue and the sun comes through and pours color in the world. Hills and fields and ruins surround us. And a long walk away is another hill town with its towers. It's like being in the middle of a painting.

The house, with its lush vegetation, lies like an oasis beside the barren fields. To the north, a stand of cypress fends against the cold winter wind, the *tramontana*. Down the hill, a double row of bushes and trees creates a shady path for walks on summer days. To the southwest, where El Greco clouds sweep above the town, is a walnut grove, beyond which a dense thicket of wild plum and brambles—a true heaven for porcupines, birds and foxes—follows the bordering ditch. Just past the *piazzetta*, fruit trees and raspberries lie in the thicket's shade.

And the house. So simple and sound. Its stone walls are full of bits of travertine, old brick, and even a handsomely carved, broken lintel from an ancient fireplace. It is made of two pieces, one rectangular, two stories tall, the other added to it, only one. The upstairs windows have heavy wooden shutters, the lower ones are laced with wrought iron grills. The walls are solidly repointed, the old clay-tile roof looks healthy, and the copper gutter pipes will outlast us all.

A broad brick walkway leads to an outbuilding dug into the hill and pigeons sit on the ridge of its roof. Inside there would be enough space for the Matra, and neat stacks of firewood along the walls. I go in. There is the lovely musty smell of wine. There is a door in the back, in the gloom, and through a small grate, I see shelves of bottles of wine, and a small wooden barrel with a glass-bulb aerator.

Marco is back with the key. We swing the great wood shutters open. Inside, the house is overwhelming. There is an intoxicating fragrance of wax, old smoke, and ancient wooden furniture. The great chestnut ceiling beams in the entranceway have a beautiful patina, and the smaller runners between them hold up pink-brown handmade tiles. The walls are whitewashed. The lower part of the house had been stables, so the floors are more recent, but the large squares of pale, handmade, uneven terra-cotta have the leathery sheen of long use. Steps lead down into the kitchen where hand-painted tiles cover the walls to eye height, a fireplace darkens a long wall, and ahead, arched glassed doors open onto another bricked terrace and the garden and the hills beyond. It's almost all too perfect. Beside the kitchen, a square eating hall runs the width of the house and its arched windows open to climbing roses. Under a brick arch we go down to a *soggiorno* with its old Persian carpet, low, commodious, down-pillowed armchairs big enough to live in, and four arched windows and an arched doorway looking onto the country, up at the town, and into the flowering, rampaging garden. And in the corner rises a huge fireplace with some strange irons that Marco says were used to keep the cooking pots warm in the old days, when the hearth was indeed the heart of the house, and one cooked, and ate, and lived beside its flames.

The upstairs has beamed, sloping ceilings and three cozy bedrooms, the biggest of which, with three exposures, is like the bridge of a ship sailing this sea of hills. And the furniture. Some of that beautiful ancient furniture is to be included with the house, all simple, country pieces, hand-planed boards with the ridges showing, hand-notched grooves as irregular as life, and a patina that sings of a thousand hands touching, rubbing, using. All those lives, still in this little house.

Back out on the *piazzetta* I sit under the glowing golden leaves of the trellis. Marco comes and sits and we stare silently at the town, the little toy houses of that dreamlike town, up there so near heaven. *"Bello davvero,"* he says. *"Quelle lumière,"* I say. What light. Then the wind gusts and parts a bush before me, and among all that green, the pink-yellow walls of San Biagio glisten.

I just stare. Then just to make conversation, I ask if the house has a name.

"La Marinaia," he replies. The Sailor's Wife.

~

I don't remember driving back to Palazzuolo Alto, except that at one point in the mountains there was a thunderstorm. Candace had gone for a walk then to the store, left a note on the table, and only then did I realize it was well after noon and I was starved. I sat outside under the racing clouds that left shadows on the hills, and gnawed the wild-boar *prosciutto,* and could not believe my good luck that here, on the other side of the world, speaking ten words of a language, groping around like a blind man in the dark,

I had somehow found the house of my dreams. I dozed off in the chair and dreamt of sailing. I guess there's only so much house a mind can take.

I awoke when I heard the Ape chugging down the road. It swung into the yard and out leapt Candace triumphantly, and her old beau gave me a great smile and waved, then spun the three-wheeler around and vanished. Candace came up the walk with two great net-bags straining. "I found fresh ravioli stuffed with truffles," she beamed.

"I found a house," I said.

Seeing on my face that I meant it, she almost dropped her bags.

It was almost dusk, too late to go back now, we'd only get to feel the house, not see it. So I described it and the land to her in every detail, every brick, every leaf, until she told me to shut up and eat my truffles before they got cold. That night we had trouble going to sleep. We went through a hundred "what if's" about the purchase, about living here, about who would we talk to and what would we do for friends. That we would be flooded with out-of-country friends there was no doubt—we had people I'd never heard of visit us in Paris—but it was the daily friendships that were hard to imagine given our shameful Italian. We finally fell asleep. In the middle of the night we awoke. "I had a nightmare," Candace said, "that we didn't get the house."

"I had a nightmare too," I said, "that we did."

Then we fell asleep again. And switched dreams. It's wonderful to sleep with someone you love; you can have reciprocating nightmares.

We left without breakfast just after dawn. The roads were empty except for a potbellied man on a *motorino*, with an engine the size of a yo-yo sputtering along, a fishing rod in its canvas case slung across his shoulder, and a tiny rectangular luggage box with his lunch.

Montepulciano glowed the color of apricot in the dawn. San Biagio's travertine walls seemed alive. Candace was incredulous. We turned down the little dirt road. There were turtledoves sitting on the telephone wires. The road was called Via Delle Colombelle, the Road of Beautiful Doves. There was no movement in the countryside until we got to the house that touched the road, just before the pond. Here a stout *contadino*, maybe fifty, with a weathered face, lively eyes, and a small-rimmed cotton hat pushed back from his forehead, was crossing the road from the hayloft to the stables, his back slightly bowed, a whole bale of hay hanging from a pitchfork over his shoulder. His arms bulged from the strain. He turned and watched us with open amazement.

Two tiny wild ducks, all black with yellow beaks, paddled in the pond along the reeds. The house was as deserted as the day before. Dew sparkled on the hayfields and the lawn. A covey of pigeons swooped overhead, rounded the house, swept up the hill toward the olives and curved off toward the pond. Montepulciano stretched across the hilltop, each church-steeple, each palazzo, each little house drawn softly in the early light. Then the sun rose, full of fire behind a row of cypresses that ran along a ridge. The air began to shake. As if in a great concerto, the great bells of all the steeples that stood against the sky sounded one by one, sonorous, tempestuous, playful, temperate, each bell with a different sound, and they swung and they sang. It was seven thirty.

"Pinch me," Candace finally said. "I'd buy this house even

if there were no house."

We walked around. The dew soaked our feet. "The house has about as much *movimento* as a shoe-box," Candace said. "But it's nice and small, and sure is well redone. And the garden is stunning. Except I'm tearing up the bloody lawn and planting potatoes, corn, and the biggest vegetable garden you've ever seen."

"I'll help you," I said.

"You sure you don't want an old ruined castle?"

"Only in my daydreams. In my heart of hearts this is perfect."

"So let's buy it," she said.

"Don't you want to see the inside?"

"You want me to die of dream-house overdose? Besides, we don't have the key. So let's go to town, eat some brioches and drink lots of coffee to make sure we are awake."

We walked up the hill to the Matra.

"Now tell me the truth," Candace said. "How much did you pay to have them ring the bells?

We walked along Il Corso, the name given to the winding, climbing, main street of town, even though it breaks into different official names along the way, and stopped in at the Cafe Poliziano, named after the town's great poet of the fifteenth century. We ate brioches and drank cappuccinos, and looked out from the great windows onto the lake. It occurred to me then that we were not only buying a wonderful house with a fairy-tale location, but we were also getting a part of this six-hundred-year-old town, its *piazzas* and churches, its *vicoli* and tiny shops. I mentioned this to Candace.

"That's a great sales pitch," she said.

"You think I'd stoop so low?"

"To get this house, I'd think you'd sell aerobics to the dead."

Then in walked Marco Lenni in search of morning victuals. We went on with our two-language confusion and an English tourist at the next table looked at us as if we had just been released from an asylum. Marco went and phoned to arrange to get the key, and he phoned another *geometra* named Piccardi, who was the *real* go-between, to meet us at the house to clarify property lines, furniture to be left and, of course confirm the price.

The caretaker, a short, well-fed neighbor named Bazzotti who had a caved-in forehead from some enormous ancient blow, met us at the house and opened up. We toured the inside and fell in love again. Then came Piccardi. Tall, midlife, good-looking, big voiced, fervently alive and boisterous, to whom nothing was impossible and everything was funny.

We laid out the property map on the dusty hood of an old tractor and Bazzotti pointed out the many corners and borders, but Bazzotti talked a ferocious dialect, so Piccardi had to translate to Italian for us. Candace, to be certain, made questions in English, I translated that to French, Marco in turn to Italian for Piccardi, and Piccardi in turn to dialect for Bazzotti. Tower of Babel.

When everyone was worn out and more confused than before, Piccardi showed us the antiques to be left. Then he confirmed the price. He wrote it in the dust on the hood of the tractor with his finger. All those bloody zeros. We countered, in the same dust with a good bit less. That was our written offer. Piccardi said absolutely no, they'd never go for it.

But he'd try.

~

We went home emotionally exhausted. We barely ate, closed the shutters on the afternoon sun and slept. Somewhere in our slumber the phone rang. It was Piccardi. He rattled on, but all I understood were the words "owner" and "millions". As for the rest, I had no idea what he said and told him so. He asked if we could meet him at the house around four. That I understood.

Driving there, we imagined everything, and exhausted every possibility.

We turned down onto Via Delle Colombelle in the quiet afternoon light. At the house on the road, a big-shouldered old lady carried two chickens in her arms, and she raised one slightly to us in salutation. We stopped at the house, full of worry. What if they've refused our offer?

Marco arrived first, sauntering casually like a man without a care, then came Piccardi in a cloud of dust, with that contented look as if he'd just saved the world. He shook hands, walked up to the dusty tractor like someone stepping behind his desk, lifted his index finger, circled something on the hood, then with an indefinable grin, said in as strange an accent as you can put on just two letters, "O.K." We rushed to look. The number he had circled was the offer we had made.

My throat tightened. Then everybody shook hands and everybody talked.

The deal was closed.

We inquired if we should leave a deposit or sign something, but Piccardi waved his hand, and Marco said why don't we sign the hood of the tractor.

Then they excused themselves and left. And we ran down to the *piazzetta*, and did a little dance, and stared in disbelief at *our* house in Tuscany.

13 ~ THE CONTRACT

*F*or the few days remaining to us, we flew, by the half hour, high into elation and low into depression. Our moods swung with the success or failure of our beggar's Italian, in achieving the tiniest of trivia like finding a doormat or buying a rake. The major things like having the power, water and telephone switched to our name —a simple procedure in most countries—proved to be Homeric enterprises that drove us to the brink of madness and made us long for the familiarity of North America.

We fell into the abyss of the infamous Italian bureaucracy. It was in a tiny gloomy office, with barricades of yellowing documents stacked against doors and windows, and we were there to procure a *codice fiscale,* a sort of financial number without which —as any dead-eyed civil servant will be thrilled to tell you—it is *assolutamente impossibile* to have your electricity hooked up or telephone connected, or indeed to purchase any object larger than a shoe. Almost. Because in Italy things are rarely absolute, and never impossible. Nearly everything can be solved if one applies some intelligence, humor, and a threat of significant bodily harm. Or in our case the magic word, *"Giornalista."* Journalist. At the mere suggestion of public scrutiny, the most comatose civil servant leaps miraculously to life, casting aside newspapers, crossword puzzles and the family photo album which he has been redoing with uninterrupted dedication for almost twenty years, and utters the word that you want to hear: *"Vediamo."* Let's see. Then the thing is as good as done. You will still have to make at least three long voyages to distant offices and wait in interminable lines but sooner or later you will succeed.

This concept of the "flexible impossible" was articulated years later by a witty and creative lady who worked for the Ministry of Finance. *"Caro* Máté," she said, sweetly calling me dear, "organized countries like Germany or America have a modest number of—for the most part sensible—regulations. But they are enforced. In Italy instead, we have an almost infinite number, many dating from Roman times, some contradictory, some incomprehensible. But we can usually, with some good will and intelligence, find a way to navigate through them. Because, *Caro* Máté, in the rest of the world two plus two equals four, but here in Italy it sometimes equals three and seven-eighths and sometimes four and a quarter. And what keeps our wits sharp and alert, is that we never know from day to day which it's going to be."

Amen.

But our true salvation lay in one word—Piccardi. We ran into him on the street during our Calvary, and he invited us for a coffee which he ingested at a throw, then, hearing about our bureaucratic woes, offered himself as savior. We moved with the speed of blind revenge. He knew everyone, everything, all procedures and their shortcuts, knew how to hurdle the "impossible" in world-record time. So he led us in full flight through dim offices, had us sign stacks of forms, each time shelling out $15 for a *"bollo da ventimila,"* a foul-tasting government postage stamp that must be licked onto any document, and told us to rest assured the house would be ready and usable on our return in the spring.

Then we all met in Florence at the office of the *notaio*, not a notary public, not a lawyer, but an official dreamed up by the Italian government to certify any fantasy anyone wishes to put on paper. The genteel owners were present, and both *geometra*s were present, and we convinced Joyce to be present because we decided that the time had come for us finally to understand what was being said, and we were there for at least three hours not because there was much to be done—it was a simple two-page contract—but because everyone in the finest Italian tradition talked all at once, and nobody listened, and the poor *notaio* almost went hoarse trying to get past the words that Joyce translated to us as "hereafter known as the vendors."

We drove back to Paris for the simple reason that our return flight left from there. By the time the plane backed up from the gate, I was homesick for Tuscany. It would be four months before we returned.

PART II

14 ~ AT HOME IN TUSCANY

*T*he almond trees were precociously in bloom as we turned into the hills towards Montepulciano. The fields, plowed bare last November, were now green with grain, and crocuses, wild daffodils and irises bloomed along the roads. Above the ditches brambly hedges of wild plum were in full white flower, as if fresh snow were packed among their branches.

We sat silently with the engine roaring, in that confusing mixture of joy and trepidation—joy because everything seemed perfect, and trepidation that we might have made the mistake of our lives. But we didn't say those words. We fretted instead about details like how will we sleep without a bed, wash without towels, cook without pots and eat without plates and live in a strange country in an empty house. We were to be left a few antiques: two *cassapancas*, low wooden chests; a *madia*, in which flour was once kept and upon which bread was kneaded; an *angoliera*, a tall triangular corner cupboard; and a small old desk; but nothing you could sleep on or eat at. We tried to visualize the empty rooms so we wouldn't be too shocked. And we worried—but only until we came over the last hill, and saw the towers of Montepulciano bathed in midday light, and San Biagio in her reassuring splendor.

Billowing spring clouds drifted over the valley. Doves swept overhead on Via Delle Colombelle. The old lady of the house right on the road, was leading a big nanny goat past the vegetable garden into a field, with a little brown kid jumping and kicking at the air. Down the hill La Marinaia snuggled in her oasis. We stopped at Bazzotti's where we were to get the key from Renata, who had looked after the house for the previous owners. Bazzotti's daughter with bewitching eyes must have recognized the car, because she jumped up from the stairs, ran inside and came back with a great steel ring, and on it the key to our house. She smiled shyly.

We drove past the pond. Great clusters of the winter's dead reeds had fallen across each other, but between them were new, fragile shoots of green. At the top of the hill, we unlocked the rusty chain strung between stone columns, and drove down. A coarse winter grass had grown tall between the tracks and whispered under us. The garden looked unkempt. Piles of dead leaves had accumulated, wind-swept, in odd places and the trellis was a skeleton of naked, leafless vines. Snow had forced flat some long-limbed shrubbery, and spring weeds had sprouted everywhere. The house too seemed forlorn. With the windows and doors shuttered and peeling, it seemed to be waiting for a new life.

We unlocked the big wood shutters, and pushed open the glassed doors. An odor of wood, and stone, and age, cool from the long winter, wafted into the sun. We went in and groped for the light switches but the power was shut off, and so I went around and opened the inside shutters. I blinked in confusion. The big eating hall was indeed empty but down the steps in the *soggiorno* loomed shapes of objects I didn't expect to see. Besides the antiques, there were the four down-pillowed chairs and the old Persian rug, and among them a low travertine table. The kitchen too had some surprises: a tin garden table covered with a faded tablecloth, and two wood garden chairs, and on the shelves a few pots and pans, and plates and soup bowls and cups.

Candace called from upstairs. I went. In the big bedroom was a double bed with pillows and a cotton cover. Candace stood at an open wall cupboard. On a shelf were sheets and pillowcases and towels, all neatly ironed. Someone besides us, someone we barely knew, had worried about our coming to an empty house. We threw open windows and shutters and let the sun-warmed, spring air stream into the rooms and expel the cold of winter.

We went back out to get our luggage but ended up meandering in the garden, looking at the tiny leaves sprouting on rose bushes, smelling the pungent fragrance of the white-flowered *lentaggine* that formed a hedge along the walk to the outbuilding, kicking piles of leaves, wandering into the hayfields, ending up on an eastern bluff where the sun-warmed air ghosted up the slope. Here, a few years later—we didn't dare dream of it then—our son, tousle-haired and in short pants, would spend hours in the fields holding with all his might, his kite soaring in the warm summer winds that swept up the hillside.

We were standing there, staring across the valley at a pine-shrouded ruin, when we heard a car on the clay road on the ridge. It turned down our drive, stopped in the clearing above the house, and out stepped Piccardi with a fruit crate packed with jars of preserves. He explained how from his window in town he saw our shutters open, and how his wife, who has a passion for putting up preserves, was worried that we'd come to an empty pantry, so there were cherries and plum jam, and whole plums and apricots, and artichoke hearts in olive oil. And a bottle of olive oil from his trees, of course. He asked if all was well, and we dragged him inside and showed him all the things the previous owner left. He said simply, "*Normale.*" Which of course it wasn't. Then he left and told us he'd check in again tomorrow, then raised dust along the road as he drove back to town.

We shelved our jars in the pantry and began to settle in. The suitcases we lugged upstairs, and we were putting some things away on shelves and hooks when the second visitor came. It was Bazzotti. He had come in through the open front door without knocking, and only when he was well inside the house did he call out loudly, "*Permesso?*" May I? Tuscan style. In one arm he had a wicker-shrouded demijohn of wine, and in the other a paper bag whose contents seeped grease through the paper. It held a string of sausages he had made himself, and a half-loaf of bread. He talked with his small eyes squinting, straightforward, unsentimental, and his great, sunken gash sometimes blushed. Renata, his wife, had meant to look after the house as she had for the previous owners, but she has not been well as of late. She sent these things not knowing if we'd had lunch. Then he left, chugging up the hill in his Cinquecento.

"It's beginning to feel like Christmas," Candace said.

We laid our treasures on the table. Then we began hunting for gas valves to light the stove, and breaker panels to turn on the hot water, and a switch for the furnace which we couldn't find, so we lit the fire in the kitchen. We sat by the fire and roasted Bazzotti's sausages, poured his wine, munched Piccardi's wife's artichoke hearts, and poured more of Bazzotti's wine. We ate and drank some more until the sun went down and it got dark, and we forgot that we still hadn't found the furnace. So we showered in the cold house, started the fire in the *soggiorno*, dragged down the mattress from upstairs, and laid it on the old rug before the flames. We put on the sheets, puffed up the down quilt we had brought from Paris, turned out the lights, listened to the enormous silence, and watched the distant, comforting lights of our fairy-tale town.

We slept. The deep, dreamful sleep of those at ease in their own home.

~

A flood of sunlight and concert of birdsong woke us, and the tapping of a beak on tin. Somebody was building a nest in a drainpipe. We went to the windows. To the east, the town was silhouetted against the early light, each tower etched in black, each rooftop solid dark; you could sense the mystery of its streets in the shadows. To the south, beyond the tall wild roses, San Biagio stood solid and comforting. To the west was the hill of lavender and rosemary and the pomegranate bushes and the wild hedge full of birds. We dressed and rushed outside as if going somewhere, then ambled aimlessly around. Candace announced that she was starving and went in to get a piece of bread, but the bread had been left out overnight and had turned to stone, so she ate some plums from the jar with her fingers. Then she said she was still hungry so we drove to town to shop.

We stopped at the Bazzotti's and saw only his mother, short and smiling, and we thanked her profusely for the gifts of yesterday, and we're not sure to this day if she had any idea of what we were saying. Then we said our good-byes and drove up to town.

It was a normal Wednesday morning, but to us it felt like

the most festive day of the year. Outside the town gate, under the ilex trees, was a balding man on an Ape with a small workbench mounted in the back. He sat on a stool and sharpened knives that people had brought down. But now he was finishing the last one, and people stood around and gossiped, so Candace went to over to him, pulled out her Swiss Army knife and said, *"Per favore."* The little stone whined and sparks flew. Then Candace came back proudly. "First contact," she said.

On our way to the gate, we edged over to the low stone parapet and looked down into the valley, just to be sure it was all real, just to be sure La Marinaia with its little island of green was still there. It was. Then we invaded Montepulciano.

Montepulciano was built for humans not for cars, so the main street was just wide enough for conducting daily affairs, evening promenades, and small festive processions. No outside traffic is allowed, so we walked in the middle of the quiet street that from beginning to end at the Piazza Grande is but a ten-minute walk uphill, and much less coming down. We passed the little gnome guarding his *cantina* full of bottles and jars of tourist ware. He looked at us, smiling expectantly. We wanted desperately to tell him that we were locals, dammit, not tourists, but we were too shy, so we just walked by. He glared.

Across the street from him was the cobbler's shop with a handful of old boys sitting on old chairs against the wall. A hundred steps inside the gate was the first store we needed. It, like so many in small Tuscan towns, was a store of many faces, a general store of sorts without the hardware. There were pots and pans and plates and *grappa* glasses, and doormats, and electric fans for the summer heat and electric heaters for the winter cold, and wedding gifts and baby gifts, and what we needed most: an espresso maker.

And for the kitchen stove, big ugly tanks of propane that gave one hernias, so the son of the earnest-faced *signora* who owned the shop would bring them to house in his Ape. Oh yes, La Marinaia; my son knows the place.

Next door was another mixed store: postcards, cameras, binoculars and the film we wanted. The door was open. But there was no one there. The cameras and binoculars lay on open shelves. We called out, *"Buongiorno!"* There was no response. We felt like thieves being in a store alone, so we went back out onto the *corso* and stood conspicuously away from the door in the middle of the street. We waited. Nobody. Then we heard steps and turned. It was a sizable butcher with his apron smeared along his two thighs where he always wiped his hands, and he said, *"Sta per arrivare dal parrucchiere."* He's coming back from the barber's. So we waited, assuming he'd gone for a quick errand. And waited some more. Only when the youngish man arrived, with his wavy red hair freshly cropped, did we understand that he had been gone for a good while, with his shop's door ajar, and cameras on the shelves. Yet he was a careful, dedicated young man, we were to discover: the official town photographer. We would often see him at concerts and plays and town events, always with a camera, recording impressions of his town for posterity.

We found out later that his empty shop was not unique. Tuscans are a social lot, and apart from necessary errands to barbers, banks and a *merendina* at the local bar, they often wander off to another shop to chit-chat, or to the churchsteps to get some sun, or to the corner to talk with the *vigile* or the sweeper, or the cobbler's to sit with the old boys against the wall.

We went a few more steps, past an antique store, a tiny jeweler, a barber, a shoe store and a bar—of which we had counted three since we entered the town—to a tiny fruit and vegetable store across from the church where Christ lay full of thorns and the pincushion Madonna stood with her chest of daggers. The fruits and vegetables were laid out neatly in the street in wooden fruit crates. Braids of red-skinned onions and garlic dangled from pegs; small barrels were filled with beans and lentils and chick-peas; big jars with sunflower seeds and nuts; and crates with figs and dates and gnarled ginger root.

We had three shopping nets from Paris with us, and we asked for a kilo of this and a kilo of that, blood oranges and clementines, tomatoes, potatoes and carrots, onion and tons of garlic. A quiet lady, the owner, asked where we were staying, thinking we were here on an off-season farm holiday. We beamed. Then we explained to her, that we were, as of yesterday, locals, having bought La Marinaia, and she laughed and said she used to go there as a child because the priest lived there who taught her catechism, but in a hurry, because he liked to go off hunting on Saturday afternoons. So she chose what we asked for and set aside the slightly bruised fruit and gave us only good ones.

Then the bags were full and our arms stretched, and Candace was still starving, so we found the bar Cafe Poliziano, and stuffed ourselves with *spremuta* squeezed from blood oranges, and brioches, and *caffés*, and Candace said, "This sure beats the hell out of shopping at A&P".

~

Thirsts and hungers quenched, we hit the street again. We still needed the butcher, the baker and a place to buy cheese. We saw a lady carrying a big round loaf in a paper bag, and Candace asked her where she'd bought her *pane*, and she pointed down the twisty street past the little *piazzetta* where on top of a building some huge ancient figure in a carnival outfit swung every half hour and struck the world's dullest bell.

We searched the curved little street awash with fresh-bread fragrance, but we found no baker, and ended up back on the *corso* again. Breadless. But oh that fragrance. So we looked and looked, and by that point I would have settled for a loaf of Wonderbread for it was getting close to noon and we were nowhere near done shopping. We had seen three grocery stores on the way, miraculously small, wedged into nooks, all of which had a couple of loaves of bread, but Candace was going to find The Baker, by God, or eat no bread at all.

There was something wonderfully personal about those hole-in-the-wall grocery stores. They all sold the same few things: pasta, milk, the inescapable tomato sauce, a bit of *prosciutto* and salami, fresh mozzarella, cheeses and eggs, and a few household goods—that's all there is room for in a store the size of a closet. But they all had at least a few clients at a time, who came to do more than just shop: they were there to linger. It seemed to me—and this was confirmed through the years—that they, just like the old boys at the cobbler, were in the small stores for company. There was an impersonal supermarket near town, but they—just as we—avoided it like the plague. And so they would spend twice the time, going from butcher to grocer to baker, waiting their turn, and enjoying a bit of gossip about the weather, or the kids, or how bad the school is, or how lazy the mayor, or how if the *vigile* gives you one more parking ticket you'll make him eat it, or how's your back, or what did you do Sunday, or how can you be so stupid as to step off your own stoop and break your ankle. Perhaps small things, but small things make a life, and a town, and a livable society.

129

So anyway, there we were with all the bells tolling, up the *corso* without bread. We panicked. We slipped into the first small shop and bought two kinds of cheese and asked for the most common of objects: matches. No matches here, the lady said, you have to go to the *tabbaccaio*. But as we stood there speechless that a grocery store has no matches, in came, of all people, The Baker, talking away, with a wicker basket of bread that he dumped unceremoniously into a wooden bin. Still chatting away, he departed.

"Follow him!" Candace ordered. "I'll catch up with you."

"How the hell will you find me?"

"It's a small town."

So I tracked the baker. We passed the bell twanger and twisted down the side street where we had been before, and there was his little store, behind a door with a curtain over it. Heaven. Crates full of big round Tuscan loaves, and bean-shaped Tuscan loaves, and whole wheat loaves, and flat things that looked like crushed slippers and hence were called just that, *ciabatta,* and *ciaccia* that crispy hard-baked wonder, slick with olive oil, and buns. And that fragrance. I kept buying things just so I could stay and inhale.

Then we raced to the butcher. And waited. Italians don't buy meat; they extract it like dentists do teeth; slowly and painfully. Now it's true that the gleaming white-tiled butcher shops are a place of wonder, with great shanks of *prosciutto*, and miles of coiled sausages, and tiny moldy sausages of *cinghiale* hanging there, and skinned rabbits dangling with a bit of fur left around their bunny feet and tail, only—so I was told—to prove they're not the neighborhood's stray cats, and long, skinny-legged, racing chickens called *ruspante* that spend their lives happily in the great outdoors, running from dunghill to dunghill and back again. They dangled there with feet and legs still attached, their crests cavalierly to one side. And of course there are slabs of lamb and veal and pork-ribs, pigeons and quail. So it is hard to choose and easy to stare, but the most time is consumed not in silent contemplation, but in the interminable exchanges between the average client and the butcher, one of which I noted years later:

Butcher: Carlotta, what do you say?

Carlotta: I'm not saying a word. Every time I say a word I'm wrong. Ask my husband.

Butcher: How is he doing?

Carlotta: Top of his form. Lungs strong as ever. After I left, I could hear him yelling at me even past the church.

Butcher: Cook him something good.

Old Lady Bystander (butting in): Cook him some rat poison with castor oil. Then when he's back on his feet he'll be thankful he's alive.

Carlotta: I'll probably overcook it and he'll throw it in my face and *I'll* end up on my back. Give me something, Augusto.

Butcher: A nice guinea hen.

Carlotta: I made that yesterday.

Butcher: Roast pork.

Carlotta: Hates pork. Says it reminds him of my mother.

Butcher: Veal then.

Carlotta: How much veal?

Butcher: A couple of nice slices like this.

Carlotta: That's too much. Thinner.

Butcher: Like this.

Carlotta: It'll break his dentures and he'll blame me for that too. Thinner.

Butcher: How thin?

Carlotta: Just thick enough to fold over the rat poison.

By the time our turn came, we were weak with hunger, so we bought up what was left in the store, and just in time, because the bells tolled one, and Tuscany ran for the shelter of the kitchen table.

The Matra creaked under the load. Candace lost all self control and began gnawing on a sausage and a loaf of warm bread. At home, we unloaded and quickly set the garden table under the trellis, where the honeysuckle climbed and a few now even bloomed, and great bumblebees buzzed among the blue flowers of the rosemary on the slope. And we poured the olive oil over tomatoes and slices of mozzarella and basil, and attacked the sausages and olives, and drank Bazzotti's wine. Then we carried the mattress back up to the pitched-ceiling bedroom, opened the shutters so the sun blazed in, and with the sunlight all over us, had our first big, festive, soon to be traditional *pisolino*. Nap.

~

I awoke in the kind of daze that says please let me sleep on for another hundred years. Candace was wide awake staring at the enormous beam and the clay tiles overhead. The sun was low, the walls of the town already aglow. I tried to snuggle and drift off again, when her voice of reason announced, "Someone has to go and hunt down the furnace."

It was true. We were sure that it existed, we had seen the radiators, even opened their little valves and saw some water drool out, so we knew they weren't just fake, installed to impress company. But we had searched every nook in the house and had found everything larger than an ant—everything but the fugitive furnace. So we rose and hunted. We moved rugs and furniture to see if something lay in waiting beneath the floors; we searched for an attic but of course there was no attic, the sloped ceilings were in fact the roof; and we fought. We fought because Candace had the preposterous idea that we go look in the outbuilding sixty feet from the house, where no one in there right mind would ever put a furnace, and where—bloody hell—it in fact turned out to be. There was a little room cut into the hill, with a steel door, which at first glance held crumbling garden furniture, but beneath that deceptive facade lurked a huge German monster of a furnace. We flicked an industrial-looking switch on the wall. The furnace roared like some U2 rocket lifting off for Coventry, and Candace yelled, "Run for the shelters!" That night we had heat. And later that night as we sat in the warm and silent house, we had to admit that whoever restored the house had class, for keeping that roaring beast at a good distance.

After we lit the furnace, we began a sunset walk around the garden when on the *piazzetta* we ran into another visitor—a pretty blond girl of eleven. She stood holding a plate, covered by a fresh cloth. I recognized her from the house right on the road, where I had seen her wobbling on a much-too-big bicycle. She held the plate out to us and said in a tiny voice, *"Sono Eleonora Paolucci. Lo manda la nonna."* I'm Eleonora Paolucci. Granny sends it. Candace took the gift. Without a further word and not listening to our thanks, she said *"Arrivederci"* and scurried up the steps and hurried, sometimes skipping, home along the road. We laid the plate on a stone wall and took off the cover. There was a great fig leaf below it and below the leaf a slab of very soft, very fresh goat cheese, blinding white, sitting on another fig leaf. This was the most moving gift of all. So simple. By a child, from a grandma, whom we had never even met, and smiled at only once from a distance, the one with the chickens in her arms.

15 ~ NONNA AND
THE WITCH

We were finishing Nonna's goat cheese with plums from the Piccardis on the *piazzetta* next morning, when the realization came over us that, the bed, four chairs, four antiques and the rug notwithstanding, we were living in a basically empty house. I recalled having seen a place at Monte San Savino with a scribbled sign that said *"Trovaroba"*—which translates somewhat awkwardly into "thing-finder"—and had an intriguing blend of simple antiques and junk. So we ate and left.

Past the pond we stopped at the Paolucci's.

Paolucci was in his small vineyard beside the house with his stout, square-shouldered mother, the Nonna, who smiled seldom, but when she did it was with her heart. And for the first time we saw Rosanna, Paolucci's wife, sturdy and serious but with a wry humor that we would discover only later, when our Italian expanded beyond hello, thank you, and good-bye. They were all tying vines to the old wires with bits of hemp. Paolucci came over first and we made awkward introductions and shook hands. He had thick square hands, as hard as wood. Then Rosanna came and did the same. But Nonna just stood in the distance at the vines with her big glasses and watched. We had to go to her. Candace thanked her profusely for the *formaggio di capra*, and Nonna replied, almost offended, that it was *"Di nulla."* Nothing. And she said a few more words with immaculate clarity of which we understood little, and that scared Candace because she had been cramming Italian all winter. We later learned that Nonna—we called her that thereafter, call her that even now, and she seems to like our having adopted her without ever asking—had her immaculate clarity in a ferocious dialect using some words that we have not heard since.

In fact, she seemed to have developed a few words all her own. It might have been in her early days alone in the fields near Montechiello when she was only seven, the oldest of five children, and began to go out, alone into the hills, with a scraggly flock of sheep to find them richer grass along the edge of woods, or down along the *fossi*, the deep, wooded ravines. And she would spend her days alone, tending them, talking to them, to no one, to the universe.

So Nonna talked to us in her broad skirt, and in her cracked and tattered boots that she wore without socks and unlaced. And I stood there listening, not understanding, never for a moment guessing what a great part of our lives she was to become, with her gentleness, her strength, her humble, wise advice. And how I would dread, each time that we returned from a long journey, and rolled down the dusty Road of the Beautiful Doves, that one day, Nonna would no longer be there.

~

We drove north over back roads into the hills we knew.

Knowing the country, and having a history there made us

feel confident and at home. So much so that we completely suppressed the fact that we knew not a single word that related to furniture. Thank God for that, or we would have probably turned back.

Few things are as much fun as hunting antiques in Tuscany. The antique stores are—or at least were then—as mysteriously obscure as Neri's operation, and just as often you could find something in an old shed of a farm and pass an enjoyable hour gossiping and haggling with the *contadino*.

The *trovaroba* was open. The front of his dilapidated building looked as if high tide had left the remnants of a hurricane. Piles of old pots, olive oil vases, ancient beds, rakes and shovels, harnesses and saddles, tables without legs, legs without tables, chairs and bits of chairs, church bells, church pews, half rotten candleholders and wholly rotten yokes. Then out came the *trovaroba* himself. He was a big-boned, big handed man, his simple face beaming with a child-like honesty, and eyes that openly solicited your friendship. Furniture stain had found a permanent home in the creases of his hands and under his nails. The sleeves of the old wool jacket he wore—much too small for him—were riding happily up toward his elbows. Candace started pointing at things and asking "*Quanto costa?*" when a brilliant light went on in my head. I gave the same speech I gave Neri about an old house etcetera, but I replaced "looking for" with "have."

Then I added, *"Molto semplice."* His eyes lit up, *"Roba rustica di contadino,"* he said. Poor farmer's things. He guided us into the bowels of his cavern. Here the tide had piled items to the ceiling. There was everything from old altars to hay carts and ceramic dolls' heads. We dug. I felt like a Saint Bernard searching through an avalanche for survivors. Then I found a beautiful leg. Of a chair.

I exhumed the rest. Small, hand hewn, with a handwoven, coarse-grass seat. Then I found another, sort of similar at least in idea, the wood all polished from wear, perfect for the kitchen. We chatted as we dug, learning new words by the minute, through the *trovaroba's* patient explanation of objects and their uses, the types of woods, the types of joinery. We were on our third chair, halfway into the pile and sweating like pigs, when a shrill voice shattered our sanctity, *"Roberto!"* Followed by a volley of equally shrill words. Roberto's face darkened. *"La moglie,"* he said gloomily. The wife.

She appeared. Her hair was straight, dyed as black as night, furtive eyes, a mouth that never shut, and a frozen grin that said, "Smile while I de-bone you." Roberto explained who we were and what we were looking for, while *la moglie,* baptized Maria—and why the priest wasn't excommunicated *on the spot* for the sacrilege I'll never know—smiled and smelled blood. Ours. Her hands began moving faster than her mouth, pulling, tearing, yanking—mostly from the pile we had discarded—the most heinous obscenities God has ever let man get away with making. We kept saying no, no, no, but poor Roberto's Malediction just kept digging like a truffle dog, and shoving the things at us. And she must have been short-sighted to boot because she'd come so close to me I could count her fake eyelashes. And she wouldn't stop. Imitation Louis XIV chairs, brass plated tin tables, a stuffed fox, on and on. Candace, at first polite, began to get murderous and she wasn't even hungry, until finally, after about a hundred "no's" she lost her temper, picked up two of the heinous things Maria had thrust at us, and said calmly in English, "Maria, this stuff is more frightening than you. Now go away!" And she put the two obscenities firmly in her hands. Maria stopped breathing. She stood there with the little Eiffel tower and the chipped plate with the image of the

Queen. Then she left. Roberto looked at Candace, as grateful as a puppy. She had a friend for life.

It was a good dig. From it came four hand-hewn farm chairs, a sturdy chestnut table for the kitchen, and a *madia* made of cherry. All needed cleaning and rewaxing but Roberto promised to have them done at no charge and delivered next week. And we found some wonderful odds and ends: an old copper sieve and copper pots, our very own chestnut-roaster with a closeable lid, an ancient wrought iron single bed for a guest, some worm-eaten candle holders, and the most vital thing for a perfectly empty house— a carved, double yoke for mules. But best of all we found a friend to whom we returned often over the years. And over the years even Maria mellowed.

~

Just as the sun was setting that evening, we drove up to town—our town—and walked arm in arm along Il Corso. We walked with the locals, as the locals have done every evening for centuries, except that all the locals had each other to talk to and we knew no one. Until we saw Piccardi. He came bustling out of the *palazzo* where he had his offices—with their towering vaulted ceilings, frescoed elaborately with idyllic landscapes—and greeted us as if we were long lost friends. We told him how wonderful his preserves were, told him we discovered the furnace, talked on and on until we had exhausted our vocabulary and were forced to say good-bye. And that was our first social evening-stroll on the *corso*.

So we were pleased with ourselves as we marched up the *corso* to Marco Lenni's office to retrieve San Filippo. He was happy to see us—Marco, not the Saint; the Saint couldn't give a damn, just kept staring at that bald skull in his hand. But when we took him home and hung him on a nail on the big wall of the eating room, he seemed content to be there and peered out of the corner of his eye at his new domain. And with that one nail in the wall, we staked our claim to La Marinaia.

16 ~ MOON OVER TUSCANY

As we looked for a place to hang the Saint, it became obvious that the inside of the house was in desperate need of repainting. It would be a simple job; the house was small, all the ceilings were unpainted, coarse, clay tiles, the kitchen and bathroom walls were mostly glazed tile, so the whole thing should be a snap. If we started early in the morning, we could finish half by noon. We ran to the hardware store for the five gallons of latex we needed. But in Tuscany things are not that easy. It's impossible to ask for something in a hardware store without being confronted with, *"Per che cosa?"* What for? Then comes the advice. Not just from the owner, but from everyone else present. And the advice does not come in simple phrases like this brand covers more or that one covers less, it comes connected to endless anecdotes, about how my brother-in-law tried one, the fool, and in the end had to replaster the house, or how somebody used another and fell off the ladder and spent a month in bed. And so on. So we got home at noon. With two buckets of lime.

Now lime eats flesh. I was told that plainly when I was ten, whitewashing a pigsty on my uncle's tiny farm. And later I had read a murder mystery where the body was cast into a lime pit and never seen again. Not even a bone. So we dressed like mummies, donned sunglasses and began to paint. Not with rollers like modern people, but with enormous whitewash brushes that weighed a ton. By evening my arm hung limp like a rag. But my flesh was intact. We finished in a week. When Roberto arrived with the furniture, the house was blinding white. And smelled like a freshly whitewashed pigsty.

~

On the third day of our whitewashing we were coming back from an errand in town, rolling slowly through the olive groves and vineyards where there was the eternal unhurried movement of those who worked the land.

Paolucci was up in a big olive tree on a narrow, hand-hewn ladder, pruning with a curved pruning saw and shears. And Nonna, wrapped in a kerchief against the spring wind, was gathering up the olive fronds into bundles for the goats. Rosanna was coming from behind the stable, with a wood tray of small onion plants that she was taking to her *orto* to plant. In Tuscany *orto* means strictly and uniquely a vegetable garden, a thing which everybody has, and another word, *giardino,* is used for a garden of flowers and shrubs. But it's not used very often for few people have more than a few mostly potted flowers, because who in their right mind would spend great effort growing things you can't eat. Rosanna came right to us and informally put the tray on top of the car, leaned in the window and asked how things were after five days in Italy. She said in all seriousness, "You must speak good Italian by now."

We laughed. Fluently.

~

Little by little, we took hold of La Marinaia or perhaps she took hold of us. With each piece of old furniture we found, with each old painting we hung, we claimed her for our own. And we attacked the garden. The former owner must have loved Kentucky, for on two sides of the house there was lawn to the horizon. Our first task was to lay waste to it—to destroy *il giardino* and create an *orto*. Paolucci beamed as we told him in pantomime about our plans. The next morning we heard a machine chugging near the house. It was Paolucci rounding the curve past the outbuilding, fighting for all he was worth with a giant rototiller, that lurched and bucked, and tried its damnedest to catapult him to the moon. Without us having asked, he drove his little beast out onto our back lawn and ripped it to shreds. I watched in horror. Candace beamed with joy. When Paolucci finished his massacre, he turned off his machine, sat down on a wall, lit up one of his outrageously stinking cigarettes and studied his handiwork. The yard looked as if it had been bombed. All day we loaded the mangled turf into the wheelbarrow and with endless voyages back and forth, dumped it in a hollow in the thickets. The birds loved us. They'd never had home delivery of worms before.

The next step was to hoe the dirt. Candace, excited at the prospect of planting a vegetable garden, decided to skip her *pisolino* and start in right after lunch with a hefty Tuscan hoe. So out she went in shorts and T-shirt, her skinny limbs glowing white after a long winter, and waved happily to me as I headed toward the peace of sleep.

I had closed the shutters to keep out the sun, and was drifting off when I heard the first deafening thud. Then another. It sounded like an ax cutting a tree. Thud. I leapt to the window. Candace raised her monstrous hoe then brought it down with all her skinny force: thud. Under the thin layer of soil was clay. Hard as rock from a month without rain, clay. The stuff that bricks are made of. The only difference between bricks and our backyard was that bricks are brittle. Our yard was cannonproof. After making a few scratches with her hoe, Candace, pouring sweat, leaned against the wall and tried to catch her breath.

She stood there forlorn and my heart was breaking for her, when like some fairy-tale knight on a rusty orange charger, Paolucci sitting proudly on his little tractor rattled around the corner, the steel tracks clanging merrily, and hanging attached behind it, a five-clawed monster called *il ripper*. Without even slowing he barreled onto the clay and harrowed it to bits. Candace watched in unbounded admiration. Now instead of having one colossal brick, we had a thousand the size of the average head. Not exactly loam. But Paolucci was not disheartened. He told us unequivocally that the bigger chunks of clay had to go, and that he could bring with the huge shovel-like attachment on his tractor, very fine silt from the ditches below. And so the next day we did our soil transplant. We took the clay down to the hollow, and in its place dumped sandy, crumbly soil. Then for two days Candace and I spread it, raked it and cleaned it, and turned it into beds, with stomped-down paths between them. When Paolucci showed up a few days later, he stopped surprised. *"Bel lavoro, ragazzi."* Good work, kids. And with that stamp of approval from the *contadino* of *contadino*s, we felt accepted as budding farmers in Tuscany.

~

Over the weeks that followed, Candace turned the old clay-mine into a verdant *orto* that fed us all year. At the weekly outdoor market in town—which everyone called *la piazza* because it was held there until the town outgrew its walls—we bought flats of tomato plants, and three types of lettuces, bunches of young onions tied with string, and tiny plants of cucumbers, zucchinis, eggplant, celery and peppers, and melons. We hauled them back to the Matra, and crammed them in between shovels, and hoes, and a roll of fencing to keep out the long-quilled porcupines that could mow the garden to bare earth in one night. Then we went home and we planted. And we seeded radishes and beans and parsley and so much arugula that it grew into a jungle. And with water from the pond above that was ducted underground to the house, there grew the most wondrous vegetable garden you would ever want to see. We did it all with Rosanna's constant advice, and with Paolucci's present of a cart of manure from his *stalla*, that stunk the place to high heaven for a week, but yielded plants I had only seen in gardening magazines.

Throughout the spring and summer, Franco and Rosanna would shower us with surprises. We would come home from fur-niture hunts to find a long A-frame made of sticks onto which to tie tomatoes, or our onions and garlic beautifully braided and hung up under the eaves, or the arugula thinned, or a bed nicely hoed. And when we would thank them profusely for their most generous help, they would invariably shrug it off, saying they had some time with nothing to do—an impossible lie—and anyway we're neighbors.

We finally managed to return some favors by helping them for a few days with the haying, and after a long struggle convinced Paolucci to accept payment for at least his tractor labors. He grumblingly consented, but always charged us for fewer hours than he'd worked, so we had to argue or just slip in a few thousand more liras among the bills. He never counted them anyway.

~

One uncommonly warm spring evening, with the stone walls of the house and the bricks of the *piazzetta* giving back the heat of the sun, we decided to have dinner outside. It was a light affair of olives and cheeses and a salad, so we donned sweaters and jackets, loaded up our arms, and set the table under the trellis. We lit two candles and watched the lights of the town twinkle like a string of amber pearls.

The corner of the *piazzetta* where the trellis and table were was cut into the hillside, which was held back by a stone wall. At the end of the wall was a brick fire-pit. We set a small fire blazing. There were no lights on inside the house or out, and only the flames and the candles lit the night. Our shadows danced on the walls, where so many shadows must have danced over the centuries. Far on the ridge, a soft glow from the dusty window of Paolucci's stable shimmered, and when he finished feeding the cows, even that went out. At the pond, after a long winter buried in the mud, the frogs started up a tentative chorus.

We ate and drank, warmed by the glowing coals.

Candace had toasted some bread over the coals for *bruschetta* and was coming back to the table when she stopped and stared behind me at the sky. "Drink down your wine, Chum," she said. "You won't believe your eyes." A soft glow lit her face. I turned.

I expected to see the dark town with faint lights against the sky, but instead saw the lower part of town ablaze with orange fire. The houses and the towers were black against the light, and some houses glowed, others were swept with flames, and the flames shot through the belfry of the steeple and the bell hung a stark black, for behind the steeple and behind the houses glowed the enormous orange moon. And as we watched in disbelief, the great orange ball started rolling up the hill behind the roofs, behind the towers, like some giant opera set come to life.

And from that night on at each full moon, we would be in our *piazzetta*, bundled up in the fall and spring, moving to keep warm in winter, lounging lazily in the heat of the summer night listening to the deafening frog chorus from the pond, watching the colossal moon lay siege to the town.

17 ~ A TUSCAN EASTER

We guzzled and gulped Italian. We were bound and determined, even at the cost of our sanity, to learn the language that everyone around us spoke with such infuriating ease. We studied Italian language books. We read Italian newspapers underlining words we didn't know, looking them up then writing their meaning in the margins. Unfortunately the papers were all full of politics—which not even the Italians understand because there are over four million major political parties—so we read about Grand Prix racing because it was easier to follow and the people looked less crazy, and came away with translations for such life-and-death daily words as airfoil, posi-traction and triptonic. And we read Eleonora Paolucci's cast-off *Teleromanzi*, a sort of comic-book-soap-opera with photographed bimbos and hulks, where we picked up such essential Tuscan countryside favorites as, *"Oooooh, ooooh, Tesoro. Baciami, baciami, bacia tutto il mio corpo,"* which means, "Ooooh, ooooh, Precious. Kiss me, kiss me, kiss my whole body."

We even did the unthinkable: bought a television set, and watched the *Telegiornale*, the news—the Italian version of reality, a flexible amalgam of fresh headlines, old footage, and clips from Steve McQueen movies.

English we avoided like the plague. When we saw the odd tourist in town we turned our heads; at dinners with mixed-language friends, we spoke only our barbaric Italian; and even when just the two of us went to restaurants, we spoke Italian to each other with errors and accents that must have given indigestion to every local in the room. We even took a two-week course in town, at which Candace excelled and I broke all records for lack of retention. But we survived. We picked up phrases left and right, from shopping in town, visiting friends, and getting Vitti the plumber to come and sabotage our furnace.

~

Giovanna had carried out her double-barreled threat—she had left her third husband and moved back to Italy. And she was giving us the best Easter present *she* could think of—coming down from Milan for the weekend.

We waited for her at the small Chiusi station, the train blasting out of the darkness, and she burst down the steps and during hugs said, "If you don't get me an Easter present I'm getting back on the train." So we stopped off at the first bar and got her a giant chocolate Easter egg, the kind that blanket Italy at Easter. Then we headed homeward.

A thin fog was rising from the hollows of the valley and was creeping after us as we wound upward through the dark country-side. The Matra's yellow headlights turned the night into an eerie hue. We hadn't seen Giovanna since November, so she chattered on feverishly about her new job, her new life and her new dreads in Milan, and how thrilled she was to be there. Then, in an unsettlingly atypical personality swing, she not only asked us about our new life—the house, the neighbors, how we were adjusting—but actually *listened* to our responses. Italy was changing her.

We rose out of the fog into a bright starry night with a thin moon rising over the Apennines. It was almost ten and we were all starving for dinner, but decided on a short walk around Montepulciano just to get the flavor of the town at night.

There are five enormous gates through which you can enter the town wall, and we chose the one near La Fortezza, the town's inner fortress, that with its surrounding quiet gardens and ancient trees occupies the highest, most tranquil part of town. The narrow streets were silent and deserted, lit only faintly by the amber lights from the wrought iron lanterns that hung now and then from the walls of houses. A bell tolled ten. We ambled about following tight, gloomy *vicoli,* up and down darkened stairways, in and out of cul-de-sacs that sometimes ended at rusted gates, sometimes at a chapel and sometimes in a tiny *piazzetta* dense with potted plants that threw eerie shadows on the walls. We stepped noiselessly through the arched entrances of *palazzi* to catch a glimpse of their monastically still courtyards, and their arched *loggias* supported by thin columns, and damp carved stone wells.

Behind the darkened *comune,* we found our way to the brick parapet and looked out past the roofs of the town. In the valley below, the dim light of La Marinaia shone like a tiny boat adrift on the darkest sea. Then the fog closed over her, and the town was alone on the ocean of the night.

Somewhere in the town, a heavy wooden door was shut, then everything fell silent once again. Walking back to the Piazza Grande, no one said a word. A church bell tolled ten thirty. We began a descent when we heard the footsteps. A shuffling of feet.

We slowed. The shuffling grew louder. And louder. With murmurs. We stopped. We had lived in New York. We knew not to ignore signs of danger.

In a silent town, with stone walls all around, where an echo can be so much louder than its source, it is practically impossible to discern with certainty the direction of sounds. We looked at each other for suggestions, but it was too dark to see expressions on faces. We heard somebody cough. Then another cough. Then shuffling. Then not a sound. Giovanna grabbed my arm as the first black-hooded, black-caped man rounded the corner. Then another. And another. Then two more black hoods and capes but with torches, held low, at menacing angles as if looking for something to set aflame. Then came six more black-hooded shadows, pall-bearers, carrying the corpse. The corpse lay dignifiedly unmoving. Its naked, yellow limbs glowing lifeless in the flicker of the flames. Its face waxy white. The hooded men sagged under its weight. Then a short priest all in white. His hands folded in prayer, eyes at the ground. Then solemn people holding candles with colored paper cups slipped halfway up them to keep the hot wax from dripping on their hands. They shuffled past us as if we were invisible ghosts. Then came a group of women carrying white lilies. Then four more men, unhooded his time, pallbearers as well, but the woman they were carrying was upright, the Madonna in blue cape, with solemn face and her chest full of great daggers to show her pain. Behind her was the whole town, old and young, some with candles, some without. And they wound up the hill to the steps of the cathedral, and there, led by the priest, turned and went inside.

"And that, pals," Giovanna said, "was our cheery version of the Easter Parade."

~

"Accidenti alla brutta Mamma della Madonna." Damn the ugly mamma of the Virgin Mary, Paolucci roared in his raspy voice. It was the next morning and we were going for a walk, showing Giovanna the valley when passing the Paoluccis' barnyard, we saw Franco trying to shoo with his green hat a half-crazed, long-limbed hen toward Nonna. Nonna stood beside the road, in her weathered boots and the kind of sleeveless, small-flower printed dress-apron all Tuscan woman wear for housework or the garden. She stood there with a shovel raised over her shoulder like a warrior ready for battle. We had asked the Paoluccis the week before if we could buy some of their free-range birds: chickens, guinea fowl, pigeons, whatever and whenever they had extras to sell. They assured us that the next time they killed and cleaned something for themselves, they would do some for us too, but not until then, because it was a lot of work to boil water in the great wood-fired cauldron under the little roof, for plunging the dead chickens into before plucking. But now the fire was crackling under the cauldron and the next day being Easter Sunday, I had a feeling we were about to witness the execution.

Chickens aren't called dumb for nothing. The stupid chicken Paolucci shooed ran right toward Nonna. She uttered a few clear words, perhaps a prayer, then she swung. The shovel flew its deadly arc. *Clang.* The chicken staggered. Nonna muttered last rights, tapped it gently with her foot so it fell onto its side, then placed the shovel handle across its neck, gave us a look that seemed to say, "what a life," placed her great boot atop the handle, and goodnight.

"Buon appetito," Giovanna mumbled out of her hearing.

Then Paolucci singled out the next victim, and the scene began to unfold itself again: brutal, vital, as old as Chicken and Man. *Clang.*

Franco came over to us and we made introductions, then he told us they could do some birds for us too, and they could hang them up for a day to age and we could have them tomorrow morning.

"*Perfetto,*" Giovanna said and her face lit up, having instantly converted the chicken from victim into food. "Then we can have fresh bird for our Easter *pranzo.*"

"You won't need the bird for *pranzo,*" Paolucci said, "because tomorrow you're eating with us."

And that was our first formal invitation to their house for a meal.

When we came back from our walk, Nonna was sitting in the barnyard on a chair, a small glazed tub at her feet steaming up her glasses, and behind her the great cauldron steaming even hotter, and Rosanna plunging dead chickens into it. And in Nonna's lap was one dead, long-legged chicken, minus most its feathers, that Nonna had plucked and flung into the dirt. And behind her on rusted spikes in the wall hung a whole flock of clean-plucked birds: chickens, pigeons, guinea hens and a duck, their feet tied and flung over the spikes, their heads dangling toward the mud below.

"So when can we have our cadavers?" Giovanna asked, and everybody burst out laughing and Nonna's chicken slipped and did a chicken-dive into the tub with a splash.

~

Easter Sunday lunch at the Paoluccis' was not a feast, it was a banquet. There were the five of them and three of us, so the two kitchen tables were pushed together, set, and the fire blazing, and both the wood-fired stove and the gas-fired stove at full blast, every inch of their tops covered with pots and pans, and both of their ovens full of loaded baking trays. Paolucci was as clean shaven as the Pope, all slicked out, hatless, his bristly hair combed, coming from his *cantina* with a pair of two-liter bottles of wine, ushering us in, wishing us *Buona Pasqua.*

We gave Nonna the bunch of Easter lilies we'd brought, and she looked at us through her glasses and Candace said later she saw tears in her eyes. Nonna had been accustomed to giving all her life; being thought about by near-strangers was not in her expectations.

We ate.

We started with two big trays of *crostini,* small toast cut from a baguette-type loaf, with four different spreads they had made: one of *porcini*, one of chicken livers, one of tomato and basil, and the last one of tuna with capers. That was enough to fill us. Then came the pastas. One at a time. Forever.

And Franco kept pouring wine for us all. Carla, the eldest daughter, who had turned twenty-five that year, kept snapping orders at him and he seemed to have had almost enough, until Carla, being the perfect hostess, went to pour mineral water for everyone, a nice gesture, except that she forgot that she had set the table with the water glasses upside down, and now, while she was feverishly directing her dad, she was pouring water with great precision all over the table. And we all broke up and laughed and laughed, and her little sister Eleonora laughed until she cried.

Then we dug into the first pasta. It was home made—what a stupid thing to say, of course it was homemade! *Everything* was homemade! Even the damned chickens! They were delicate little crepes made by Carla, stuffed with ricotta and spinach and then baked in the oven like lasagna, and they tasted like heaven. Even Giovanna, who, justifiably, fancies herself a great cook, rolled her eyes. And we drank. And we talked and talked—us mostly with our hands. Then came another pasta. *Tagliatelle* with rabbit ragu. Spicy with tomatoes. I think I swooned. Then came another pasta. I couldn't believe my eyes. It was handmade *pici*, smothered in bread crumbs that had been stir-fried in olive oil. When I was a kid in Budapest, it had been one of my favorite dishes. After the third pasta, Candace said she was so full, she was about to lose consciousness. Giovanna and I thought we were about to die. So we drank some more wine.

The wine and a bit of rest must have had dissolved all the pasta, because when the three trays of meats arrived we didn't even gasp.

We were by now used to the loud conversations but at that point something serious seemed to explode between Carla and Franco. Franco yelled in anger. She yelled back at him, back and forth they went, and Candace and I couldn't understand a word, but it was obvious that some serious family drama was at hand. Candace leaned to me and said, "I think she's leaving home." As the shouting reached fever pitch, we asked Giovanna—who was eating calmly and making small talk with Nonna—what tragedy had occurred. She looked at us as if we were nuts. "What is the topic?" Candace insisted.

"The salt," she said.

"The what!?"

"The salt. He asked for the salt, she said he had it, he said where, she said behind the bread basket, he said he couldn't see it and she said that she'd get it for him. Period."

"So why were they yelling?"

"Because, my dear," she yelled, "we are in Italy!"

No one even blinked.

There was roast pigeon cut into small pieces, baked in the wood oven for two hours so there was just a parchment-thin crisp skin over the gamy meat. Then there was wild-boar stew, and of course the finale: roast lamb. And roast potatoes that Candace somehow ate by the pound, and shredded salad well salted, Tuscan style. And wine. The Paolucci women drank very little, meaning that the four of us had sipped away about a liter each. Over two hours. And two pounds each of food. Then came *il dolce*.

We had brought a great fruit tart that Candace and Giovanna made. It was coals to Newcastle. Rosanna brought out her own *tiramisu*, a creamy thing full of coffee, which is why it's called "pull me up," and Carla had baked a *crostata di albicocca*, a crumbly apricot tart, and of course there was the inevitable *colomba*, the traditional Italian Easter cake, an uniced thing the shape of a dove. Then came resurrecting espressos, then of course brandies and *grappa*. The Paoluccis kept insisting we drink the *grappa* because it is a *digestivo*; it helps with digestion. It also puts you in a profound state of merriment, and lets you forget that you're about to explode. So we asked Franco if we could have a tour of the house and surrounding yards, for although we had been here almost three weeks, we had yet to see a real live Tuscan farm in its entirety.

He was thrilled to oblige us.

~

The Paoluccis' house is named Pallazzo dei Diavoli, the House of the Devils. Nobody knows for certain why since it's a few hundred years old, and nobody knows exactly how old it is. But lore has it that there was a Satanic altar up in the attic, and it is said that the priests talk quietly among themselves of secret rites, devil worship, strange offerings found buried in the walls, but they come and bless the house every spring anyway, just as they bless all the other houses in the parish. (If you want, they'll also bless your car.) So anyway, the Devils are all rumor except for the altar, whose base is still there. I have seen it with my own eyes.

Their house was built as a *casa padronale,* which means that its dwellers owned the land and house and also other houses. So it is much more lordly than a regular *podere,* which had stables down below and living quarters above. Theirs, instead, has three polished travertine steps leading into a broad long hallway that divides the house in half. To the left are three enormous bedrooms, all heated, more or less, by stray heat that sometimes drifts in from the great fireplace in the kitchen, across the hall. In the winter there is sometimes ice inside the windows. They sleep well.

To the right of the entrance is the door to the enormous kitchen which is also dining room, living room, sewing room, ironing room . . . you name it. Past the kitchen door is the door to the devil's attic, and beyond that, a door and three steps lead down into a *cantina* of a hundred fragrances. Here are kept the many shelves of preserves, aging *prosciutto* hanging from the beams, strings of sausages, braids of onions and garlic, potatoes, apples on a reed-mat, and demijohns of wine that have been decanted from the large barrels.

We went out. Nonna was sitting in a chair beside the steps in the warm sun. The sky was cloudless. Just a bit of wind. Such silence. Except for the ducks in a row waddling below the steps, loudly quacking.

"*Domani piove*," Nonna said. Tomorrow it rains.

Giovanna asked her how she knew. She said, "*Quando le anatre cantano, le piogge cadono.*" When ducks sing, the rains fall.

Franco led us behind the house.

This is where their farm really begins. Across from the *cantina* is Paolucci's favorite space, the *stalla* with four cows and a couple of calves nudging their mothers' udders. This building oozes a fragrance of hay, and cows, and old brick all mingled together, a calming smell—a smell so full of life.

Franco loves his cows. He's up at dawn feeding them, carrying those bales on his shoulder from the hayloft, across the deserted, dusty road. Then he cleans out the straw and cowdung with a pitchfork onto a big flat wheelbarrow that Pasquino, his boisterous brother-in-law, made, and wheels it out to the dunghill where the chickens and pigeons are anxiously waiting. In the evening, before closing up for the night, he repeats it all again. And between those two times, while he's out working in his olive grove, or vineyards, or fields—he seldom touches the *orto*, or the chickens, for that is women's work—he will wander in a couple of times a day, just to check the cows, make sure all is well. This he calls "*governare le bestie,*" governing the beasts.

Across from the *stalla* is a second *cantina* for fermenting and aging, where vats and barrels sit on massive wooden stands.

Between the *stalla* and *cantina* is the *forno*, a giant, dome-shaped brick oven, where, at one time, the *contadini* from the surrounding farms would come to bake their bread or on feast days mountains of roast meat and pastry. Enormous faggots of brittle-dry broom turn it into an inferno for a while, and when they burn down, almost ashless, the bricks are white from heat, and hold that heat even until morning, more than long enough to roast a lamb or an army of hens, or pizza enough for fifty.

Nowadays it is lit mostly for an evening of pizza with friends and family, or for Rosanna's special *dolci* at Christmas and *caroli* at Easter, but every time it flares and we are there, an atmosphere of celebration fills the air, everyone chipping in, hauling, lighting, carrying, shooing away the cats, pulling the trays out with long-handled lifters, then poking, checking, pushing, scorching fingers, yelling it's done; it's not done; it's burnt; it's raw; if you're so smart why don't you cook it; because I don't cook charcoal; and then everything turns out fine.

Beside the *forno* is the witches' cauldron, where the dead chickens dive, and where in summer Rosanna and Nonna and Anna, Franco's enormous and enormous-voiced sister, boil the hundreds of jars of tomatoes and jams, to put away for winter.

Then comes the barnyard. There is a small granary, a shed where an ancient machine chops hay for the cows, then a low, two-room pigsty. In one are two young mud-stained pigs, frolicking, snorting, blissfully ignorant of that frosty day next winter when the yard near the cauldron becomes a butcher shop, and they miraculously metamorphose into *prosciutto*, and sausages, pork chops and spicy head-cheese. In the second sty is a sow the size of a Cinquecento, flopped over on her side, so pregnant with little piglets that her belly lies beside her like an udder.

Paolucci opens a gate made from the old headboard of an iron bed, with wire for hinges and a cord for a latch, and we saunter into the yard behind the house that faces the valley. Shaded by three gangly cypresses, it is the kingdom of the fowl. From here they range freely, terrorizing the countryside, the fields, the ditches, the dunghill, the stable, the front steps, and in a suicidal moment even Nonna's *orto*. Paolucci must be a blood relative of Noah, for there is every type of feathered fowl here God ever created. In the coops, on the coops, beside them and in the trees, on the roof of the house, on a cart and on the fences, pecking, scratching, flapping, screeching, ambling, brooding, breeding, sleeping, chasing cats or running from them, or just practicing being dumb, are chickens and roosters, guinea hens and quail, Chinese ducks and Tuscan ducks and ducks of mixed marriages, pheasants, geese, turkeys, pigeons, doves, and a stray black bird that was injured and has since taken up residence and whistles, so like a person that I turn my head to see who's there. Then Franco shows us his three small vineyards, and his olive groves—a perfect little kingdom. We thank everyone for everything and saunter home.

That night, about midnight—just as the ducks had predicted—the skies opened and it rained.

18 ~ THE FROGS

We poured new energy into our hunt for old furniture, working on tips from Piccardi and the neighbors about which farmhouse might have what piece for sale, and where a part-time *trovaroba* might be hiding. Besides a few mandatory items, we also found unimaginable odds and ends, so beautiful, or so irresistibly useless, that only the iciest of hearts could have left them in their cobwebbed corners. But we also got to discover untravelled and beautiful parts of Tuscany. We found tiny towns, got to see the insides of farm houses at the ends of hidden lanes, and best of all, we met some of the most charming characters God ever invented.

One of them was called Nebbia, "fog." That was his *soprannome*, nickname. In the Tuscan countryside nicknames abound. So Don Flori, the poet-priest who was to baptize our son two years later, was called *Don Chilometro*, for his height; Scaccini's son was called *Pagnotta*, because he was round like a bun; the mayor was called *Brioche*, because he was mostly air; and Nebbia was called *Nebbia* because he was a dreamer and because as a young man he had an explosion of light, curly hair which, from a distance, looked like a bank of rising fog. He was the only man I ever met who I would call "jolly." If there really is a Santa Claus, it must be Nebbia in disguise.

Nebbia—a *trovaroba*—lives in one of Tuscany's most beautiful little towns. It forms a point in a small triangle of picture-perfect towns, within which are three castles, two monasteries, uncountable ancient ruins, and enough twisting, dusty country roads to last a lifetime. The hills here are smaller and the valleys tighter than in most of our region, so there is a greater sense of mystery. And there are no highly sought-after grapes, as there are in Montepulciano or Montalcino, so the change here has been almost glacial, and the tiny farms, called *aziendas,* have remained intact, diversified and rustic.

We approached from the east, twisting slowly on a one-lane road, paved here, graveled there, depending I suppose on the mood of the local road crew. The town has just over a hundred residents, and only one gate. The main street—there are only two others in the town—is circular, following the fortifying walls. The houses are minuscule, many with outside stairs leading to the habitations above. The street-level floors were once tiny stables but now the animals are gone, so they are used as *cantinas,* and for firewood, and to hang big shanks of *prosciutto* from the beams to cure.

We walked into the town during the afternoon *pisolino,* passing the closed butcher, the closed miniature grocer. The only waking soul was the cabinetmaker, who was out in front of his cavelike workshop, studying an old kitchen table whose legs had rotted to the knee from being stored in some dank, earth-floored place for years. We asked him where we could find Nebbia and he laughed, hearing foreigners using a *soprannome.* Then, in the finest Italian tradition, instead of giving directions, he led the way.

Nebbia had been asleep, so he appeared even more *nebbioso* than normal. He blinked hard into the afternoon sun, looking around as if trying to get his bearings in the place where he has awakened every day of his life. His voice was soft and playful, he almost sang as he talked, and he tucked at his big loose clothes and said that sure he had some odds and ends, nothing interesting though, because it was getting hard to find anything good in Tuscany. It was all in a stone shed in the country, and we were welcome to have a look, but we had to wait a bit until he fed his dog, which he had just acquired and was training to hunt truffles.

While we waited, we walked around town. The main street passed through a man-high, vaulted tunnel and branched off into a cross street that led to the town's small *piazza*. On one side rose a chapel-sized church, on another the *municipio*, whose crumbling wood shutters hadn't been unlatched for years, and on the other sides, small houses with laundry dangling from lines worked by pulleys between windows. Hidden behind tall walls, visible only through a narrow rusty gate, was a fairy-tale wild garden, full of mingling shadows and colors, with trees, bushes, plants and flowers, a brick well, and a little gazebo with an old iron table and chairs. It seemed the gardener could not decide between vegetables and flowers, so dianthus bloomed among zucchini, roses among onions, and the garlic lived with geraniums, all slightly overgrown and hopelessly entangled. It seemed a place where fables could be born.

At the edge of the town walls was a tiny *piazzetta* with a bench under blooming *acacia*, whose clusters of yellow flowers dangled like grapes and perfumed the air. There were three old ladies on the bench, one knitting, all chatting, and beyond them, wooded hills, some olives, the odd *podere,* and on a rise a steeple.

Nebbia found us and we walked back through town, past the *falegname* who was still trying to stare his crippled table back to life, and down along the road toward the cemetery, to a little two-story *casetta* in the country under huge pines. He unlocked a door in an arch so low that you had to duck to get in, and led us into the gloom. In the half-light of a single bulb on a twisted wire stood some of the most beautiful old furniture I had ever seen. There was a fifteenth-century *cassapanca*—a chest—of beautiful proportions, low, long, with four inlaid panels, black from the hundreds of years of dirt and smoke of fireplaces mixing and blending with infinite layers of wax; a church pew, sagging in the middle, its arms worn round from hundreds of years of nervous hope; a simple little table made of cherry which, because of its hardness, was worn to a patina like glass; an *inginocchiatoio*, a church kneeler, with a place not only to kneel but also to rest your elbows while in prayer; an iron bed, very plain, but with two wonderful paintings on oval tin, one set in the headboard, the other at the foot, of old ruins at twilight—like De Chirico at his worst.

Nebbia placed himself in an old armchair—he was born to sit—made himself comfortable as if in a nest, and held court. He never tried to sell us anything. He just chatted about what interested him, and what interested him was now Canada. All that space. All that wilderness, all those lakes and mountains and foggy ocean shores so perfect to dream on. And he taught us Italian, correcting us, explaining, and, after much nudging, talked about the old furniture, how to discern age, how to discern source, and how to tell one wood from another, because *noce* and *ciliegio,* walnut and cherry, were valuable, but *pioppo,* poplar and other softwoods, were worth half as much, because softwoods didn't build up that patina that was as deep and variegated as the surface of a lake.

After an hour the light began to fade in the archway, and we finally began talking about which pieces we wanted and the prices. Nebbia was asking surprisingly little, so, perhaps to his surprise, we didn't haggle, and after we settled on the church pew, the table, the kneeler, the bed with the paintings and the five-hundred-year-old *cassapanca*, he lowered the prices again for taking them all and saving him hours of bitter haggling with the bored and boring Romans who cruised the countryside and ruined all his Sundays. Then, when we said our good-byes, he gave us two old chairs, because, he said, he liked Canada.

As we walked back to town counting our blessings, a huge red sun settled in the hills.

~

Once in a while, Paolucci would untie a couple of his cows from the manger of his stable and take them for a walk as city folk take dogs. There was a kind of ritual to his outings. He would lead the cows from the *stalla*, and turn down the dusty road, always down toward open country, never up toward the town. And he would lead them with a coarse hemp rope wrapped around their head and horns, and the other end around his hand. He would lead them with their great dumb feet kicking up the dust, past the hayloft and past the lower vineyard, past the little brick house where the dark-watered well lived, and then he'd turn from the road down to the shores of the pond. Here he would drop the rope and let the cows tear at the fresh grass that grew on the bank. With his pocket knife, whose blade had been worn narrow from sharpening, he cut himself a switch from one of the elms, whipped the air to try the sound, found himself a piece of hay to stick between his teeth, gathered up the rope, gave it a yank, and was off again. He had three routes to choose from. He could recross the road and follow its narrower branch down into the tree-shadowed valley where the Scaccini brothers, the seventy-two-year-old twins with backs as straight as poles, had their fields and house. Or he could keep along the road and head into deep country toward the ruins. Or he could drop below the pond and keep below the vineyard toward our house. It was a joy to hear their flat hooves thud on the brick walk, and we would watch as they nibbled our flowering bushes and Paolucci would swear and yank the rope, and deliver a theatrical kick in the ass. *"Madonna gonfiata,"* Swollen Virgin Mary, he yelled.

Then he would set them free in our walnut grove where the sweet medicinal grass grew under the trees. He himself would sit in a chair under the trellis, sip his glass of wine—which he never allowed me to refill past the halfway mark, but to that mark I could refill as often as I liked—and talk. He loved to talk. He would talk about how it was time to find another young calf because one of his cows had an udder so full she dragged it like a plow, or why his older daughter doesn't marry after eight years of courtship with her stonemason beau from San Quirico D'Orcia, *porca miseria,* because she'll be on pension before they set a date. Or he would talk about the *Corvo Nero*, Black Crow, the nastiest woman ever born, with a mouth like a barrel hole and tongue like a whip, who would think of nothing of moving piles of rocks or small trees in the night to widen the boundaries of her fields and totally *far incazzare*—piss off—all her neighbors. And who, in the night, would drive her big ugly tractor that was loud enough to keep the dead awake, and how one time over a discussion about a ditch, flattened poor Crociani with a right hook that scratched his cornea and put a patch over his left eye for a week. And Crociani was *dolce come il pane*, as sweet as bread. Or he would talk about his youth, about how on Saturday nights they would dance at one *podere* one week and another the next, in the summers in the dirt yards, in the winter in the *cantinas* handy to the wine. And how they would head home at dawn, exhausted but bursting with youth, and how one time in the fog he rode his bicycle over the bank into a tree, bounced back and hit it again, three times before he finally fell over.

Then after a few glasses and a few more stories, he would go and get his cows, ask them if they had enough nice grass to eat, then he would coax them, cajole them, and occasionally kick them in the ass to get them to move toward the hole in the hedge and home.

~

Around Montepulciano, in the windows of the shops and cafes, we had seen posters for a *concerto* in San Biagio. It was a girls' choir visiting from Wales, and we had heard much about the spectacular acoustics of the church, so we were thrilled at the prospect of spending an evening there.

The interior of San Biagio does not stir the soul. Its high Renaissance good sense, so appealingly simple on the outside, results in an overly disciplined interior that suggests a post office or bank, but that vast dome and towering travertine walls yield a crystal sound. The concert was to start at dusk, and since it was less than a mile from the house, we walked. We followed the clay road up through the fields, then through the woods, past the cemetery, and down again to the church. The sun had set. Inside, San Biagio was almost dark. Only a faint light came down from the high win-

dows, and the rest from banks of candles. At first we thought it was
an oversight, that in typical Italian fashion the lighting for the concert had been forgotten, until we realized that there were three
times more candles than normal, and caught on to the notion that
this was exactly how the place was lit four hundred years before.
Why should it be lit differently now? So our admiration grew and
we savored the candlelight.

In all Tuscan churches there exist these racks for real candles,
in small country churches near the altar, in bigger ones under the
statue or painting of some saint. The racks resemble music stands,
with little metal clamps. The new candles are kept unlit under the
rack, and are taken by the faithful in exchange for a few coins and
placed in the little clamps and lit, sometimes in memory, and
sometimes just in hope. Near the time of religious holidays the
racks are filled with candles all aflame, and the silent churches,
glowing and redolent of molten wax, are enough to bring the heart
of the most rational atheist closer to the simple faith of those who
lit the candles.

About a quarter hour after the scheduled start, the pews
began to fill. People whispered. Another quarter hour after that—
by Italian standards precisely on time—the concert began. From
the sacristy door behind the altar, out came the girls, about thirty
of them, between thirteen and eighteen, each in white blouse and
jumper. They took their places in three tiers on the wide steps of
the altar, and they began to sing: classical pieces, folk pieces,
melancholy laments, and boisterous Italian folk tunes. Their faces
seemed to glow with the limitless possibilities of youth, and while
their exuberant voices rang in the dome, they allowed their audi-
ence, much older, to believe in those possibilities again.

We walked home the way we had come in a cloudless,

moonless night. The dome of night was dense with stars. In the
dark pond, the frogs, in full chorus, sang their reptilian hearts out.

19 ~ PICNIC AT THE RUIN

After a few weeks of living in the countryside, the languid calm of provincial life was flowing, at a trickle, through our veins. Days would pass without our using the Matra, and we came to prefer walking to town. It would take less than half an hour, including time to stop and look back out over the valley, or to sit and rest a moment on the stone bench of the shrine with a cupola below the town walls.

Those stops were predictably short, unless we stopped to visit with neighbors along the way. At Bazzotti's there was always his mother outside, washing or sweeping or tending their few flowers. Or Bazzotti, after his work was done, on a small bench in the shade, weaving a wicker basket for acorns and mushrooms, or a wicker shroud for his demijohns of wine, or making, out of twigs of erica, the brooms he used in the mornings as the town sweeper.

At the Paoluccis' there would always be Nonna in the *orto*, or hunting for eggs in the hay-loft or the bushes, or cleaning and directing barnyard traffic with her broom. Or Eleonora after school teetering on her bicycle, or Rosanna at her steady pace, commanding the whole house. And Franco would wander between chores, stopping at the front steps where he kept his glass and bottle of wine, stopping for a rest and *una goccia,* a drop, before he went back to work, *piano con calma.*

And up the road from them were the Anselmis, aging husband and wife, always grateful for a bit of company, and at the top of the road Crociani with his wife, mother, father—with the world's warmest smile—and his son Marco who was shy but would be riveted to our conversation and even our dumb questions, such as why they used willow twigs to tie their vines, and do they hoe around their olives to keep down weeds or to let in rain. These encounters would slow our journey, but they let us be part of the life around us.

And day by day, phrase by phrase, embarrassment by embarrassment, these encounters increased our Italian vocabulary. And my God did I suffer embarrassing moments. One balmy June evening, heading to see the advertised *Saint Francis of Assisi* at *cinema sotto le stelle,* cinema under the stars, we stopped at the Paoluccis'. I confidently announced where we were going, in what I thought was flawless Italian. I was met with glassy gazes. Candace, snorting with laughter, informed me that I had just told them that I was off to see St. Francis *sotto le stalle,* under the stable.

Then there was the time when Bazzotti, after seeing Candace jogging on the road, remarked in admiration that she was a true *campione,* a champion. I tried to respond with a witty remark: I said, "She's a champion all right, but only with her mouth."

Bazzotti didn't laugh. He blushed. Confused. I held my breath. Then I explained in desperation, "She talks too much."

Bazzotti thought, unreddened and began to shake with laughter. Can't blame him. For I had said, "She's a champion all right, but only with her hole."

Now, let him who can honestly see much difference between *bocca* and *buco* cast the first stone.

~

So we had become provincial, ever more content to live our lives within sight of our house, in our town and the valley. Outings to such distant outposts as Pienza, 8 kilometers away, had begun to require as much planning as a voyage to Antarctica.

At one point I noticed with surprise that I had not, for a whole week, crossed the paved road, having been content to live life even without the town. But we weren't sedentary; we took long walks in the country. We were the last inhabited house on the road; beyond us the road was all ruts before it petered out across the valley to a trail. When seeking solitude instead of company, we simply walked up our weedy drive and instead of turning left, turned right. The road dipped and curved, and we walked at a much-slowed pace, from deep into deeper silence. We left behind the vineyards and the olive groves where the sound of voices often filled the air, out into the stillness of the green wheat fields and hay. The town receded in the distance and in memory. Skylarks hovered and trilled their solitary tune. The wind rippled the wheat like long waves of the sea. The white clay of the road felt soft and gentle underfoot, and the further we walked, the slower we went, not from fatigue but from the pleasure of being there. We breathed deeply.

The road ended at the first ruin.

It was a chunky, two-family *podere* that sat on the last high point on the ridge, an ancient mass of brick and stone atop a hill of clay. The clay sagged and shifted as it turned from solid to mush during the rains, and the shifting had taken its toll over the years, a crack here, a split wall there, but all patched, so the old house stood a bit teetering, a little out of square, the doors and windows somewhat out of level, but solid. Awaiting someone's dreams to fill it with life again.

At the small pond, dense with bulrushes, the road turned into the valley. Wildflowers thickened on its slopes; pale Queen Anne's lace, deep-red poppies, chamomile and margaritas, buttercups and clover were reconquering their old domain. At the bottom of the valley, following the course of a winding stream, stands of ancient oak and poplar shaded the valley floor, and the wind brought breaths of cool air from their shadows. Next to the stream lay a long-abandoned vineyard, its poles leaning, its columns fallen, its thick, gnarly vines untied, hanging like forlorn willows. If you turn and look back from here, you see the rolling hills of young, green wheat rising like giant waves against the sky. And in a cleft in their midst, as if on an ocean, Montepulciano, sun drenched, sailing between the earth and heaven.

It wasn't always easy to cross the stream. At medium water you could jump across, but just after the rains, you had to gather fallen poles from the vineyard, and splash and get wet and jury-rig a bridge. Once across, you were in the valley of ruins. Downstream were the weed-choked walls of a crumbling mill, with its overgrown small dam, underground water chutes so high you could wander inside them. There was a welcoming coldness there during the stunning heat. This is where the witch lived, so I would tell our son on our walks years later, and his eyes would light up with joy and fear, and even more so when I snuck away, and made chuckling, witchy sounds from the darkness of a shute.

The hills all around were dotted with ruins: big, small, towerless or towered, some almost intact, some just piles of rubble, and still others, like my first dream house in Tuscany, knee-high lumps under a hill of brambles. But the best ruin of all was just up ahead.

From it you could see not one living house, not a living soul. Absolute silence. Unspoiled countryside. You could easily feel yourself in the century before, or some other one before that; after a while it was hard to tell. In the spring, the fresh colors and new growth filled you with zest and life, but in the summer, the great, moored heat bade you to be still. We came here, Candace and I, on a hot and sunny day, to celebrate our anniversary with a picnic.

This best ruin of all had a crumbling tower. It was roofless now, with one whole side collapsed. The steep, interior steps had vanished, leaving only the holes in the walls to show where they had been. The outside stone steps too had been removed; only one lay there as a witness of better days. The perlin beam had rotted in the hayloft, broken in half and come down, and the heaps of old roof tiles that came after it reddened like fresh flowers in the weeds. A fig tree had gone wild, dove in through windows, swept over roofs, burst through the walls, and bridged the sky like a jungle vine to the pigsty across the way. There was no shade other than the fig's—the trees must have been cut to make more room for pasture—so the whole valley around the ruin was open, flowing meadow. No one came there.

We set a tattered tablecloth among the wildflowers on the ground, laid out our olives and cheeses, and the small, still-warm guinea hen that had roasted beside the fire since early morning, laid out tomatoes, radishes and strawberries, all fresh from our garden. We broke the loaf of bread because we had forgotten the knife, uncorked the bottle and poured the wine, then we drank a toast in that immense silence. Happy anniversary.

Only a few birds sang below us near the stream, and cicadas shrilled in the midday heat, and the bread dried as soon as it was broken. We reminisced about all the years together, tried to recall each anniversary, laughed, and shed a tear about all the good times and the bad. Then the food was gone, and the bottle empty, and only a few crumbs and some strawberries were left, and a couple of ants hurrying, uninvited, to the feast. We were drunk with fragrance of hay and strawberries, and the wine warming at the bottom of the glasses.

"You can't see a soul from here," Candace said.

"Not one," I said.

"And no one can see us."

"True again."

"What do you think?" she said, with a mischievous smile.

"Now?" I said.

"You want to come back later when the birds are sleeping?"

She looked ravishing. The great heat enveloped us.

It was a still afternoon. Candace was asleep, wrapped in the tablecloth, its embroidered hem lying across her shoulders. Her red hair bleached lighter by the sun, her freckles in summer bloom. I had never seen her more beautiful. I felt almost afraid of being so much in love after all those years.

⌐

Saint Francis of Assisi was screened on a beautiful starry night. A screen had been stretched on a courtyard wall of the Benedictine library, built in the 1400s, overlooking the valley from one of the highest parts of town. Folding chairs—about fifty of them—had been placed on the paving stones. The lights were turned off and the courtyard filled with darkness, then a big projector whirred and the O's and numbers started flashing on the screen.

Behind us was another wall, and to our right four big arches of a *loggia*, but to our left was only a waist-high parapet, with two perching gargoyles worn round by the ages, glaring with no-longer-scary eyes, at the night full of stars twinkling all around them.

On the screen was a smiling, young Saint Francis, walking under the arches of his native Peruggia, and at times it was hard to tell where his arches ended and our arches began, and it was effortless to slip back eight centuries and walk across the *piazza* with him. It was a long film. The stars kept getting brighter and the night cooler, and chairs squeaked across the stone as people pulled them closer and cuddled to stay warm.

The valley was dark and silent after midnight. We walked through a sea of stars listening to nightingales. It was easy to see why Saint Francis had such faith.

~

Franco Paolucci was born in a farmhouse near the tiny hill-town of Petroio, which has but a single street that corkscrews and narrows as it rises. His father was in *mezzadria* with a landowner there. The *mezzadria* was a system of land-working that dominated Tuscany from the thirteenth century to the end of the 1940s, and in a few, rare places is still alive today. The landowner provides the land and house, and pays for half of all that is needed to work the land as well as half the costs of seeds and beasts. The *contadino* pays the other half and provides his long hours of sweat and toil. When the harvest comes, or *vendemmia*—the grape picking—comes, or a pig is killed, the landowner and *contadino* each get *mezzo*—half. So Franco grew up under such a system, and, like all his friends, left school after the third grade. But even though his reading is spotty and his writing slow and crude, he has developed an insight into the ways of the world, and even more impressively the ways of people. And he loves to visit and be visited, and loves to talk.

The kitchen is the soul of any Tuscan house. The Paoluccis' is dominated by a giant, smoky fireplace that is lit on all but the hottest days. In it, under the vast, clay-tile hood, are two small benches facing each other across the flames. There is a wood cooking stove in the corner and a gas stove beside that, and something is almost always simmering or baking. In the evenings Nonna sits on one of the small benches near the flames, sewing or darning or knitting woolens for the family for the coming winter. Franco sits at the kitchen table, slumped from the long day's labor, but perks up as soon as visitors arrive, and shoves the stumpy glasses toward us and pours the wine. Then after a bit of gossiping begins one of his stories.

He tells us about the years of his youth, when no family would ever undertake haying or harvesting or the *vendemmia* or wood-cutting without help from its neighbors. In May they all gathered in one family's hayfields and scythes flashed in the sun and voices rang and the fresh hay fell in great sheets to the ground. At midday the women brought the hot lunches in stacking pots to save the men a long walk home, and they all had *pranzo* together in the shade of some great solitary oak or pine, left in the field to provide a welcome shade on blistering summer days. When one family's fields were done, they moved on to the next. When the hay had dried some, it was pitched onto oxcarts up to dizzying heights, then hauled up to the yards and made into stacks. Then a feast began. At its end an accordion always appeared and they sang and danced, young and old oblivious to the fatigue of the day, sang and danced until dawn, when without sleep, without rest, they would gather up the *attrezzi* again, and walk in the breaking light to the fields of the next neighbor to pitch hay. It was enough for me to hear that story once; nothing was going to make me miss the Paoluccis' haying.

The end of May was hot that year and the hay was tall and flowering. Luckily for my feeble back there was no more scything. Paolucci mounted an ancient three-wheel mower with long open blades like a swordfish's sword, and with his hat pulled down, he cut his hay. Then it was left to dry. A few days later the hand work began. The neighbors had stopped "pitching in" long ago, so there was Franco, Rosanna, and Nonna, and in the spirit of rekindling a dead tradition, one-hundred-pound Candace and me.

We raked.

Paolucci pulled a rig behind the tractor that pitched the hay in rows for the bailer to come and bail them after lunch, but the rig didn't pitch quite everything, so the rest we raked. Candace did fine in her systematic fashion, rational, steady, calm, but not I. Like a fool, I tried to keep up with Rosanna who has a much stronger back and shoulders than I. By ten I was in pain. My back screamed. I had blisters on my blisters and the hay dust flew so thick and dry that it reddened both my eyes. But I raked on, stopping often to slug water and wipe the streaming sweat from my face. Nonna left at ten to begin preparing *pranzo*, Candace at eleven to attack the bureaucracy of medical insurance—wisely before I died—but Rosanna and I followed that stinking tractor through the hills and, as if possessed, we raked. The sun evermore burning. My shoulders turned to stone. I could barely see. My mouth was caked with hay dust. But I raked. God finally had mercy and let the church bells ring just as I was about to lie down and fall asleep, perhaps forever.

I don't recall walking back to the Paoluccis' house. The first thing I do recall was cold water running on my neck and face. I came alive enough to drag myself up the steps into the kitchen.

Then we ate. That I recall clearly. There was *lasagna al forno*, with hand-rolled pasta that Nonna made at dawn, and there was *pollo in umido*, chicken stewed in a piquant tomato sauce, and some *osso buco* and homemade French fries, and salad and sliced tomatoes and then a *crostata* that Rosanna made the night before with her apricot preserves. Then, while Rosanna and Candace cleaned away the dishes, Nonna and Franco and I eased ourselves back out into the blistering sun to set the bales. The bailing was done by a man with a machine that clattered up and down the hills, spitting tight bales of hay. But the bales lay flat on the ground, and the ducks were singing and the skies were threatening, so we dragged the bales, and set three leaning together like teepee poles, to shed the rain. By late afternoon the fields were full of teepees. I thought I was just exhausted, but then suddenly the wine and *grappa* and coffee wore off all at once, leaving every muscle immobile and numb. I mumbled good-bye and teetered home. I showered beseeching God not to let me drown, then lay down for a minute—until dawn. I slept like the dead. Except I dreamt that I was raking hay.

And that was my first day as a *contadino*.

~

A few days later, in early morning I heard Paolucci's tractor tracks clanging through the open window. They were loading the bales. I tiptoed out of bed to let Candace sleep, dressed, and went to help.

Franco stood in his rusting cart and Nonna, carrying a steel hook, walked calmly to the bales. Then, clutching the T-handle of the hook, drove it with a firm swing into a bale, dragged it to the cart, and with one rhythmical swing hoisted one end onto the gate. Franco hauled it aboard. He stacked them like bricks.

They welcomed me, joking about my unaccustomed early rise, then we went to work. I was given a hook like Nonna's and we loaded. Nonna hooked in one end, and I in the other, we swung the bales smoothly up to Franco. The first two layers we hoisted with ease, but after that we had to swing with all our might to get the bales up high. By mid-morning the valley floor was baking and each bale was heavier than the last. We had, through superhuman effort, managed to load the damned cart four bales high. We lashed the bales down with a cord, and I followed the swaying cart to the hay shed. Then we had breakfast. In the dark cool of the kitchen. *Lombo* —cured back-bacon—and green onions and wine.

Going back out I felt no pain. We unloaded then went down into the field again. I followed Nonna at her brutal pace, sometimes unsure of my footing on the coarse and craggy earth, sometimes losing my hook or leaving it in a bale. We loaded. The stack got higher, the heat more unbearable. Near noon, drenched in sweat, I stumbled after Nonna, praying for church bells, and Nonna and I had both set out hooks well, and got ready to swing up the fourth row of bales. Nonna gave it her all and I gave it all I had left, and the bale flew up and my feet came off the ground— Nonna had thrown us both in the air. But that was ten years ago. She was young then. Only seventy-three.

~

Market day was like Christmas once a week. We went to town less and less but we would never miss Thursday, when caravans of special trucks rolled in at early morning. They lined the Piazza of Sant' Agnese and the streets below the walls. As if by magic, their sides opened wide, and awnings shot out from their roofs on long, mechanical arms, and from their depths gushed fruits and vegetables, fishes, meats and fowl—alive or fresh roasted—canaries in cages and chicks and tiny bunnies, black birds that rasped *"Ciao, come stai?"* Hi, how are you? And out came shoes and boots and woolen country slippers, dresses, shirts and brassieres with cups the size of buckets, pants and hats of straw with visors or with brims, tablecloths, towels, and linen by the yard in a hundred glowing rolls, steel buckets and rakes and ladders, nuts and bolts, and irons for the fire. There were tools of every kind, and pots of every shape, and mountains of perfumes and soaps, and for the kids who would stream down the hill from school later, there were piles of nuts and candy, chocolates and toffee.

And the whole town was there, squeezing melons, trying grips of hammers, smelling flowers, choosing cheese, getting hot sandwiches carved fresh from a roasted pig that stared you in the eye. They were gossiping, bartering, laughing, arguing, "No, no, you were first; no, you; who cares, I've got lots of time," seeing who bought what, where and at what price, as if the world had stopped and no one worked and it was Mardi Gras.

And all the farmers came from every valley, washed and shaved and slicked out every market day, Paolucci and Bonnari and Carlo and the twins and fifty others like them, all in a group like chicks, all in jackets and sharp-creased pants and pressed shirts buttoned tight, gossiping, exchanging the weekly news of who was born and who died, and whose tractor broke down and whose wheat was slapped by hail, and who sold a cow for how much, "the thief," and who bought a cow for how much, "the fool," and which bachelor went to which town to find himself a welcoming lady of the night. They were the walking talking newspapers of the countryside.

On market day we brought the Matra and stacked her so full the springs sagged. Then we drove home among deserted fields where not a soul was seen until the tables were all folded, and the awnings rolled back in, and the horns of plenty closed their doors and rolled on out of town.

~

Piccardi continued with his most welcome visits, usually between lunch and three thirty, the time he reopened his office. He loved to give advice on everything from cooking to flowers, from refinishing old doors to rebuilding our chimneys. And his bubbly spirit and big voice and his rock-solid conviction that everything was possible relieved much of our anxieties as we tried to put together the jigsaw puzzle of our life. He basically adopted us as his helpless children—although he had three teenagers of his own—and Anna-Maria, his wife of the wonderful preserves, invited us for lunches and dinners of such variety and flavors that it took us months to get up the courage to invite them back.

And Piccardi found and looked after the renovation of an old printing shop for Candace to use as a studio. It was a voluminous space with a big arch and giant oak beams, that opened onto the most interesting *vicolo* in town. The *vicolo* was a wide set of curving stairs bordered by shrubs and flowers, and two trees above a great old wall throwing broad shade after noon. The windows of the studio opened onto a convent garden, with archways and roses and the serenity that only a walled garden can bring. The space was just moldy walls when Piccardi found it, and we cleaned and scrubbed it and then left for Canada for two months to see Candace's relatives, and asked Piccardi if he could look after bringing the plumbing in, to which the owner had agreed. We came back to a palace. The walls had been replastered and painted, the old wood beams sandblasted and restained, the cracked cement floor covered with Tuscan tiles, everything rewired, and a beautiful new bathroom tucked away with hot water and a shower, just in case. The rent, despite all this, remained just over a hundred dollars a month.

Piccardi also made our daily lives easier by initiating us into that vital Italian institution: contacts. He introduced us to his doctor, his dentist, the director of his bank and the parish priest, butchers and wine-makers and mechanics for our car, but his best introduction of all set off a chain of encounters that led us to our future son's godparents, the poet-priest that baptized him, and a fine friend, an English painter, all of them through introduction to a *trovaroba*, who had a sort of junkshop just outside of town.

Inaldo was a thin, mid-fifties, intense, croaky-voiced, chain-smoking, philosophizing, insightful humanist and the town's last angry Marxist. He would welcome us to his shop with open arms, and he would rave about the world going to hell, about the stupidity that was more and more in unlimited supply, illustrated almost daily at the intersection near his shop by the screeching of brakes then the thud of cars slamming into each other. And we would mull over the ills of Italy and the ills of the world, and conclude at the end that everyone was crazy so what's the use, let's go have some lunch and a little wine.

20 ~ TORO

*E*arly one spring morning with the valley in full bloom, the sound of excited voices could be heard on the hillock behind the house. I dressed and ran to look.

The hay had been cut, the bales carted away and tucked in the hay shed to the rafters, and the hayfields were cleared and ideal for roaming. The sky was clear, and the air crisp with spring, laced with the pungent smell of broom that glowed like yellow flames. One of the old Scaccini twins was standing on the crest of the bald hill, waving a great rag back and forth across the sky, like a ship-wrecked sailor signaling madly at what he hopes is not just a cloud on the horizon.

Voices came from beyond the crest, and I recognized Paolucci's, raspy and impatient, and the high-pitched voice of Bonnari who kept a big herd of cows farther down the valley. I went up to Scaccini—and couldn't for the life of me tell which twin he was—and asked what had happened. *"Un toro. É scappato un toro."* A bull had escaped. And he pointed down to the ruin beside the olive grove. Bonnari had been cleaning out the stable—

where he, as most Tuscans, kept his cattle locked up all year long—
and had brought the bull outside for a minute into a pen, but the
young, long-legged bull jumped the fence and headed off for the
libertà of the valley. Now they were trying to herd it back toward
the stable, hoping that once he smelled the cows he'd wander home
again.

Heads came popping out of the olive grove, and there was
more yelling, and rags and shirts waving, at the invisible bull that
was somewhere down below.

"*Sparito!*" someone yelled. Vanished!

"*Che sparito?!*" Bonnari yelled. "It's a bull! Not a flea!"

Scaccino laughed. Then they were all out in the open, six or
seven of them, rags held at the ready, coming toward each other,
tightening the ring around a patch of empty air. The bull was
nowhere.

"*Accidenti alla cieca Mamma della Madonna!*" Damn the
blind mother of the Virgin Mary!

General yelling, and frustration and laughter, and the circle
of men disintegrated, some wandering off, others pairing up to
exchange views on the event. Paolucci came toward us up the hill,
wiping his face with his sleeve, carrying a gunnysack. "*Piano,
piano,*" he said. He stopped beside us and rested. Then he said,
"*Ho fame. Vo' a mangiare.*" And he headed off toward his house for
breakfast. But he never got more than a few steps past the trees.

Like a specter rising from the mist, the big white bull
stepped out from the olive grove. He stood firm and magnificently white against the green. He didn't seem menacing, he didn't
seem excited; he raised his head happily and sniffed at the spring
air.

Everyone froze. Their rags hung still. They stood and

watched their quarry basking in the sun. A skylark twittered overhead. Bonnari's stocky son, a healthy, brawny lad, was the first to
leave his place. He was in the bloom of youth, and he moved slowly but without fear in a straight line toward the bull. He had his
checkered shirt slung over his shoulder looking like someone going
for a stroll, but now he slowly slipped it down, dragged it in one
hand as he'd seen a matador do once, in a movie. About ten steps
away he stopped and stared the bull right in the eye.

    "Throw it over his eyes, then he'll be calm," Scaccini whis-
pered, but even I could hardly hear him, never mind the boy.
Nobody moved. The bull sniffed at the air, the sweet smell of the
broom, the fresh damp from the stream, then he shook his head,
lowered it, and stared right at the boy. Bonnari's son moved.
Cautiously but steadily, he raised the shirt with one hand, spread
it with the other, spread it open, held it by his side in the breeze,
then shook it slightly, faithful in every detail to the movie.

    The bull charged, a vicious, violent acceleration, thundering
on the clay, kicking up the dust. The boy stood his ground. He
held the checkered shirt extended at his side, and we all held our
breath in fearful admiration, wishing, almost that we had his
courage. *"Toro!"* the boy yelled defiantly and gave the rag a shake.
The bull flew. It was a beautiful, heroic sight, and we all got ready
to cheer, ready to yell *"Olé!"* and Scaccini had already raised his rag
in sheer delight. But to the bad luck of the boy the bull had never
seen a movie, and the rag meant nothing to him: he charged
straight at the boy.

    The big, blunt head caught him square in the chest, but the
boy was young and quick and brought his hands up just in time to
cushion the blow that sent him flying through the air, over the
horns, over the bull, with his shirt tailing behind him like the tail

of a kite. The bull didn't break stride but ran on in a straight line across the ridge, and vanished over a hillock into the shadows of the valley.

The boy was on his feet, rubbing his ribs, checking his bruised hands, his battered arms.

Paolucci looked sadly after the bull. *"Povera bestia,"* he said. Poor beast. "He's going to die."

Shocked, I asked why.

"His heart will give out. He's not used to running free."

The circle of men tightened.

"Io mangio," Paolucci said. I'm eating. And he went.

"Call Cugusi!" somebody yelled. "He's got a horse. He can come and rope him!"

"Just like the movie," I said, and old Scaccini laughed.

We all headed up to Paolucci's to get a morning bite and a slug of wine. Only young Bonnari walked vaguely, dejectedly, in the direction where the white bull had vanished.

We returned to the hillock after we ate but the hills were empty and, except for the skylark, silent. A flock of starlings swept low over us and settled in the thick reeds of the pond. Then, like some *caballiero,* Cugusi, in flat-rimmed hat, sauntered on his horse up the hill toward us. The horse came prancing sideways as if it were in a show, throwing its head, tossing its tail. Cugusi sat pole-straight in the saddle, his head hard at an angle to match the horse's, and listened gravely to reports of where the bull might be. Then we followed him in a straggling line along the ridge like a bunch of motley peasants armed with rags, following their elegant prince to war.

Down we went into the shadows along the stream. The woods varied greatly there, narrowing to a few trees where the stream ran in a gulch, widening to copses where it ran shallow across a flood plain. Brambles and poplars sprang up along the banks, and now, in mid-spring, spewed their cottony blossoms, like down, across the sky. We spread out in a crescent along the woods, silent now, squinting, shading our eyes against the sun, peering into the wooded gloom for the white hide of the bull.

Cugusi reined his horse and eased it along the stream.

The horse, unaccustomed to the mire underfoot, the reek of fungus from the shadows, protested, tosssing its head. Cugusi patted its neck to calm it, slow strokes, and the horse went on, but without conviction.

Then the bull charged. We heard the sound before we saw him, the sucking of the wet ground, the snapping of branches. Then, as he hit the stream, the silver spray shot up among the green, and his great white head came bursting through the leaves. The horse, instead of bolting, froze in utter fright. Its legs, planted in the mud, awaited some kind of signal from the brain, but the brain didn't signal until it was too late.

The bull hit him hard in the hindquarters, and the horse, instead of collapsing, was lifted by the blow, airborne, comical. The bull passed around and under him, ran a few more steps but a steep rise blocked its way, so he turned and charged again. Cugusi, accustomed to herding sheep or riding in parades, sat stunned to helpless inaction in the saddle. The horse had turned and faced the bull and reared in self-defense, but barely: his hind sunk more into the mire than his front shot in the air, so the bull hit him abreast and the horse sat back on its haunches like a dog begging a bone. Cugusi was thrown wet and cursing but held the reins, and was back into the saddle before the stunned horse rose. The horse bolted for the dry hills, but the bull had had enough. It trotted disinterestedly by us all, and, as if it had lived there all its life, turned into the woods, smashed through, and out the other side. It trotted up the hill toward the solemn ruins of the valley, making a magnificent spectacle trotting free in the sun.

We went for lunch. Bonnari walked slowly after the bull.

The afternoon was a repeat of the morning. We would find the bull, the bull would charge, but hitting no one, just clearing himself a road to escape. In the late afternoon, to our surprise, he made a wide loop in the hills, at full gallop down the long valleys, more slowly on a rise, tossing his head, seeming to relish the endless space, the endless sky. Then, without urging or provocation, he made a mighty charge down toward the stream and vanished for the last time in the thicket and the shadows.

We went slowly down—only three of us left now, the rest gone home to chores. The woods were strangely silent. We didn't enter. Bonnari threw a clog of clay into the gloom, but there was no reaction. After a while we stepped into the shadows, throwing clogs into the silence ahead. Paolucci stopped. *"Povera bestia,"* he said softly. Poor beast. We went to where Paolucci stood, his face drawn with sadness.

The bull lay, like a fallen statue, on his side in a marshy green clearing, his whiteness glowing in the light that slanted in between the trunks. He lay with his legs at ease, eyes open, at peace, his head slightly back as when he sniffed the sky. Maybe it was the light—but he looked as if he were still enjoying the endless space, endless sky, the fresh spring air awakening all life. He seemed content. To be there. To never have to go back to the four-walled gloom again.

21 ~ SUMMER NIGHT MUSIC

A despot heat fettered the valley. The clay baked, the earth cracked, the air was afraid to move. The flock of sheep across the way stopped grazing and huddled under a great oak in the shade. Opening the shutter of the door onto the *piazzetta* was like walking into an oven. The cicadas were hysterical. Leaves hung limp. A little work was done in the fields at dawn, when the land was cool. When the shadows left the vegetable garden Candace left with them. *"Eva puttana che caldo,"* Eve you whore, what heat, Bazzotti said in his *cantina*; the only cool place left in his house. *"Solleone,"* the Tuscans call this ferocious time—lion sun. We closed all windows, all shutters, and the house fell dark, only chinks of sunlight came in through the cracks. We had trapped the cool dawn air and the cool of spring in the stone walls and the floors. We worked downstairs with our bare feet on the cool terra-cotta; and we napped. When the *piazzetta* was shadowed in late afternoon, I would go out and hose it down abundantly, and the air filled with a thick sweet smell of wet brick as it cooled. Then I would turn the hose on myself and come alive. Then I sprayed all the lavender bushes and their perfume enveloped the house like a fog.

We were outdoors in those days mostly in the early and late hours. We took breakfast under the shimmering, speckled light of the arbor. Lunch was reduced to salads or sun-warm tomatoes and fresh basil from Candace's garden, with diced, cold mozzarella, and we ate in the cool twilight of our kitchen that faced north. For fruit and our espresso we returned to the arbor again, only to feel the heat—enormous now even in the shade—and see the light quivering in the valley and on the stone walls of town. For dinners we prepared cold pastas or that most wonderful Tuscan dish, *pan-zanella*, bread salad, made from leftover bread, thinly sliced purple onions, chunks of tomatoes, basil, cucumber, black olives, and garlic, with balsamic vinegar and olive oil. It's wonderful chilled, and excellent with chunks of tuna and young red wine.

We had our evening meals outside with candlelight, watching the assault of the moon upon the town, bathed in the tumbling fragrance of jasmine in bloom, and the sweet smell of the hot fields giving back the sun. And after dinner, there was music and theater and dance, for in July and August the hills from Montepulciano to Pienza are filled with concerts and festivals, in towns and in castles and sometimes in moonlit fields.

Montepulciano has a two-week festival called *Il Cantiere*. French horns blare in the cathedral, folk songs in the streets, accordions in the *piazzas*, oboes and guitars in courtyards. It is wonderful to sit in a new place every night—in an Etruscan tomb listening to a flute, or to an entire orchestra inside San Biagio, or watch in the blacked-out Piazza Grande as a Japanese troupe in silken war-dress emerges one by one swirling from the shadows, from doorways, from archways, from the well, filling the medieval square with color and with light.

Then there's *Teatro Povero* at Montechiello about six miles away. It's a tiny, perfectly kept walled town of about a hundred people, with a leaning watchtower that a Finnish family restored years ago. Here they have folk theater, literally written and performed by the people of the town, in the *piazza* at night. It is usually a story about their countryside, the changes, the losses, the extinction of one life and birth of another. We sat in awe at the dramatically lit *vicoli* and the walls of town, and the people, none of them actors, portraying their lives, their hopes, their fears, their dreams, in the embrace of the moon and the stars and those ancient walls. For us the story was more personal still. This was the area where Nonna grazed her childhood sheep, and because we understood little of their thick dialect, we had to invent much of the play for ourselves.

Then there are the festivals of the *Unità* in all the towns. Tables and long benches are put together in a garden, with pastas and roast meats made by the local women. We went with all the Paoluccis to the one in Pienza, and afterward in that picturesque Renaissance square, between the cathedral and the *palazzo* and that beautiful well, there was a band, one of those that plays everything from polka to reggae, and everybody danced—kids with kids, kids with *nonnas*, a baby with her doll, a bigger kid with his dog. Torches flamed in their wrought iron brackets in the walls, just the way they did four hundred years ago.

Perhaps the most remarkable was the concert at Castel' Luccio, a small, lonely castle in the arid Val D'Orcia. It is still lived in, and every year, late in the summer, there is chamber music in its courtyard. The space is intimate, seating only sixty people, but the accoustics are miraculous. We listened to brooding Kodály and etherial Vivaldi under an indigo sky, in a warm wind punctuated by the flight of bats, and chamber music never sounded so good. That was only the beginning. When the concert was over, we went into a garden of great trees, and soft grasses, and a *vasca*, all of it lit by torches and candlelight, and candles floating on little rafts on the water. And here at white-linen-covered tables, under a big moon, with the old volcano silvering in the moonlight, the owners of Ambrosia, one of Tuscany's best restaurants, served a dinner that made you want to live forever, if only to return there every year, one balmy August night.

22 ~ MOON DOG

Out of blissful slumber that comes in the utter silence of night in countryside, I awoke to the sound of a dog barking. It was after three. I got up and stared out at the moonlight on the hills. It was Manetti's hunting dog, at the little *podere* whose lands started below our walnut grove. We had walked by there lately, when we took a shortcut across the fields on our way to the lower part of town. Manetti, about forty, unmarried, working at construction, living with his old mom who ran their little farm, had a nickname, *Duro*, which literally means "hard," but in fact refers to a brain into which nothing penetrates. The year before he had been up high on a scaffold, carrying something, when he tripped or slipped and plunged head first to the concrete floor below. He broke his shoulder but the head was unscathed. This year he was installing a steel beam, securing it from a ladder, when the beam unsecured itself, plunged down on his head and back and sent him flying twelve feet to the ground. His ribs cracked, his arms broke, but his head wasn't even scratched. But after this latest mangling, he was slow moving around, so the poor dog was locked night and day in his pen, and at night, enveloped in the misery of his existence, he barked.

In the morning I went over. Nicely. We had talked, Manetti and I, a few times in his dark wine cellar, sipping a glass of wine, about his broken bones and wild-boar hunts, and why his walnut trees were twice as big as ours, and I had talked to his widowed Mamma about her ten-year-old, much-sliced haystack, and her pigeons and her well. A sweet old lady, and she must have been a dazzling beauty as a young girl. So I went over, calm and gentle, if a little red-eyed.

Their *podere* was nondescript and partly crumbling. She was down in a lean-to beside her stairs, scrubbing clothes with a bristle brush in a concrete sink with a rippled concrete washboard, scrubbing, rinsing, slapping, wringing, then soaking again. *"Buongiorno, buongiorno,"* pleasantries, chit-chat, how's your son, has he fallen from the church steeple today, all smiles, a beautiful old woman. Then I mentioned the dog.

"Oh, that *maledetto,"* she groaned. That cursed one. "It kept me up an hour during the night."

"Me too," I said. "Why don't you give it a slap?"

"You can't hit a hunting dog."

"Why not?" I said.

"Who knows."

"Why don't you put in him in your shed at night?"

"He'll eat the chickens."

"In the stable."

"He'll eat a lamb."

"In the house."

"He'll eat me!"

"Give him some sleeping pills!"

195

"Sleeping pills for a dog? What am I, a millionaire?"

"I'll pay for them."

She put the soaked shirt in a wet lump on the washboard, leaned on it so hard the water squished between her fingers, raised her gentle, peasant eyes to mine, gave a little smile, and said, melodious and kind, *"Non mi rompere i coglioni."* Don't bust my balls.

23 ~ NIGHTWALKER

*B*y mid-summer, the vegetable garden seemed bent on taking over the universe. With Paolucci's sandy loam and first-class stable dung, and Candace's zealous predawn and afternoon dedication to the garden hose—which belched malodorous swamp water from the pond above—lettuces turned to bushes, tomatoes into trees, zucchinis into mutants and eggplants and melons into objects of dread.

When the heat set in, Candace was up at dawn, in her shorts of the *campione,* hoeing, hacking, thinning and weeding, the sweat running down her skinny limbs, determined to keep us healthy from her garden even if it killed her. That was on the north side. On the south, there were the fruit trees. One morning, without warning, everything was ripe. The huge fig tree above the *piazzetta* was laden with a mass of nectar-dripping figs. The plums, apricots and peaches were of the richest purples, pinks and yellows, and as if to certify the ripeness, swarms of birds and bees attacked from every side, pecking and sucking in desperation, as if the weather forecast called for winter after lunch. Then there were the berries.

The strawberries wove themselves into a mat, the raspberries lunged at the hedge, and the currants and gooseberries turned deep-yellow and rich-red overnight.

We struggled with the garden, and after lunch, with the shutters closed, we slept. One day the pond water stopped running. Giovanna was down for a visit, lying in a garden chair, dressed in a bikini bottom, browning in the sun, when a blood-curdling curse rose among the vegetables. Candace roared that the bloody hose was dry. I shouted back that this was a physical impossibility; the water came from the pond that was fifty feet higher than the garden.

"Can you please kill each other quietly," Giovanna said, "I'm on my holiday."

Candace yelled that if I didn't fix the water, the whole garden would shrivel up and die by sunset, so off I went in a state of total confusion to try to determine why, today of all days, God had decided to turn off gravity.

Our pond was across the road from Bazzotti's house, and I went armed with pliers, a bucket, some wire and a pipe wrench. It was Saturday, Bazzotti's day off from tending to the streets of Montepulciano, so he sat on his bench in the shade, whittling a new handle for a shovel, and watched with bemused interest as I struggled up the hill in the sun.

"*Mettiti giù,* " he said, making space for me on the bench in the shade. Set yourself down. I did, and explained to him the reason for my journey.

"It's too hot to be in the sun," he said. "The heat'll kill you. But then if you don't fix the water, your wife will kill you."

"*Preciso,* " I said. "She's a champion killer."

"*Preciso,* " he said. "We'd better have some wine."

He shuffled off to the *cantina* in his slippers and sleeveless undershirt, pushing his round belly before him. He came back with two small glasses and a bottle of white wine he had just decanted, the bottle already streaked with beads of condensation from the sweltering heat. He poured, and we drank. In the heat the wine went straight to our heads. Then we went out into the sun.

The pond was choked by a wreath of dead and verdant reeds. The dead ones fallen at all angles, the fresh shoots pole-straight toward the sun. Together they were impenetrable. What was left of the pond in their midst was green with algae. Bazzotti had helped install the water system, so with a worn sickle he hacked at the tall weeds on the high point of the bank, and found the little cement well. He pulled off the lid, revealing a two-inch plastic pipe interrupted by a T, and a big ball-valve sticking out of it. He opened the valve and it sucked a bit of air, revealing the dry, dark hole. "*Secco,*" he said. Dry.

"What a surprise," I said.

Bazzotti chuckled. He liked to be kidded.

From the valve, the heavy pipe went in one direction down into the pond, and in the other down the hill to our garden. Somehow the siphon had been broken and the water was no longer being sucked from the pond. We went to work. With the sickle, Bazzotti slashed and bushwhacked his way through the reeds, slipping and cursing, toward the water. I cleaned the valve and tightened all the joints, then joined Bazzotti down in the muck. We found the end of the tube with a filter at the water's edge in oozing mud. We cleaned the filter then I went up the bank and yelled.

The house was a good two hundred yards away, and a few months before I would have been much too embarrassed to raise my voice in public, but now I bellowed across the valley until

Candace came around the side, and Giovanna with her whiteness glowing came around the other side, and I yelled for them to close all the taps. We bucketed water to refill the whole length of empty pipe through the valve, then roared at Candace and Giovanna to open all the taps, and flung the end of the pipe into the slimy water. Candace held the hose up to show me a surge of water spouting out, and then they screamed. Frightened at the sound, I ran down the hill. They were standing awestruck, holding the hose and staring at the ground where the water was spewing wriggling mounds of tadpoles.

"Great invention," Giovanna said in disgust. "Prefertilized water."

~

That night the heat never left the valley. It stayed in the *piazzetta* and the hills well after dark, and we ate dinner late by candlelight in the arbor, surrounded by a full chorus of frogs, and the inebriating fragrance of cut wheat sweetened by the lavender in bloom. When the air moved, the scent of garlic and parsley rose from the bowl of fresh seafood salad. The moon was past its fullness, rising near midnight behind the steeple of the monastery of the nuns, and a small owl in the vineyard gave a high-pitched welcome to its light.

The candles had burned down in their holders, and the wax hung in breeze-blown, frozen streams. When the flames guttered, we sat quietly and let the moonlight wash over us.

Giovanna, worn out by the sun, got up, bid goodnight and vanished into the darkened house. Candace lay back against me, and before long her breathing was deep and even, in the first moments of sleep.

"Paradise," I heard her dreaming. "Bloody paradise."

When she too went to bed, I cleaned away the dishes, slowly, lazily, luxuriating in the warmth of the summer night. I turned off the lights, but on a sudden impulse, instead of climbing the stairs to bed, I went back outside. The moon had drifted clear of the roof-reefs of the town and was sailing unimpeded now, in open sky. The night was alight. I walked down to the outbuilding, heading I had no idea where. I turned up the hill. Long cypress shadows ribbed the white clay road, and I was lost in contemplation of that ghostly pattern, when I had my first encounter of the night. I forgotten that nights are full of life, or perhaps it was the beastie's size that threw me, or its careless, lumbering gait, like some old lady returning from the market loaded down. Its surprisingly long, white quills quivered in the light, like a stack of small arrows lying flat, pointing aft, menacing no one. Then she disappeared into a cement drainage pipe that ran below the road. I had the night to myself again.

At the top of our road I turned right, toward solitude. The valley before me was dark except for moonlight. After a while I turned and descended toward the darkness of the stream. There was no road there, just a tractor trail, two bright white stripes of clay. The fields on either side had recently been furrowed, and the sharp-edged clods of clay threw jagged shadows on each other. The once-gentle fields now seemed as forbidding as a desert of stone.

The fox leapt. His eyes glowed. He must have been watching me for quite some time, because the place he leapt from had been in my line of vision since I turned off the road. I saw him leap across the road, then across a hollow and stop again. He watched me. He stood maybe a dozen steps away, gazing, head raised, calm, like one who owned the place.

He finally left, unhurried, keeping to the tractor trail rather than the inhospitable footing of the jagged clay, moving slowly as if in deep thought. At the ridge, he turned back for one last look, then was gone.

I stepped off the trail onto the clods. They were impossible footing—the peaks were sharp, the tilts varied, the distances between them difficult to judge. I fell but kept on going, I don't know why, perhaps under the influence of that moonlight. It was as if I were learning to walk again. I struggled ahead descending slightly, until all around me, from the dark gully to the horizon of the rise, there was nothing but the crags of clay, cold white, almost glowing.

I felt disoriented from all the swaying and stumbled on straight down the hill to where soft rounded shadows loomed. I knew the place, yet nothing seemed familiar. I heard a gentle murmuring and couldn't imagine what it was. Things rustled above me in the shadows. At last I recognized the sound of tumbling water. An angled form emerged from the half-light: the mill. Sounds of movement inside, signs of life and the sound of rushing water in the chutes. Bats fluttered from the mill. The night was changing, and here was a new light spilling in the darkness. I turned uphill. After a while I saw Scaccini's house. I hurried by. A rooster I knew crowed restlessly, and chickens around him cackled softly. I hurried home before the light.

24 ~ DON FLORI

*L*ate that summer, just as the invasion of visiting friends ended, swarms of hornets laid siege to our chimney. We didn't notice until some of them flew out of the fireplace and zigzagged through the house. We could hear hundreds of them buzzing up above. I told Candace to be calm. Eviction was easy. I'd light a fire, good and smoky and drive the nasty little bastards out of there. I got lots of newspaper, crumpled it well, piled it in the fireplace, then to create lots of smoke I covered it with layers of fresh-cut weeds. The flames surged and smoke billowed and I called to Candace to step outside the kitchen and watch the buggers flee. She went. After awhile she called out, "Where's the smoke?"

"In here!" I yelled choking, and stumbled out with smoke billowing after me.

"You showed them eh, Chum?" Candace said lovingly.

Hornets aren't dumb. They had dammed up the whole chimney with their nest. Not a whiff of smoke was getting to them. The only solution would be hand-to-hornet combat.

Whenever I cut weeds or grass, I use a dense black netting

the size of a sheet to drag the stuff away. Now I put on Candace's wide-brimmed straw hat and draped the black net over me, tied it at the waist, taped the holes at the arms, donned leather gloves, taped the wrists, donned rubber boots, taped the openings. I must have looked like the Mad Widow from a homemade horror movie. Armed with crumpled newspaper and matches and a long stiff wire, I put a long ladder against the house and climbed toward the buzzing din. It was toward evening and the swarm was settling in for the night, so I tiptoed over the roof tiles, stuffed three of the four chimney holes with paper—I was taking no prisoners—lit a crumpled paper in my hand, shoved it in the last hole and with my wire rod rammed it down toward the nest. Things flamed and sizzled, smoked and popped. I smelled victory. I stuffed in more burning paper, and a greasy smoke spiraled from the chimney along with a few frantic hornets. The rest buzzed their death-buzz below in the flames. I was doing a little victory dance on the roof with the next flaming paper-ball held high in my hand, when I heard a polite voice right below me, *"Mi scusi. Signor* Máté?" There was a policeman on the walkway.

I scrambled down, began to explain, but got embarrassed, so I tore the tape off and a glove and offered him a handshake.

"I have brought your *permesso di soggiorno,*" he said. The permit to reside. Then he opened it and searched it for something. He looked at me, mystified, tried to look through the black netting at my face, studied the details of my costume with care, then asked with exaggerated politeness, "Excuse me, but what country *are* you from?"

~

We went to the home of friends, Gianni and Monica, in town for

Sunday lunch. He wrote books on philosophy, she was a painter, and they lived in a small house above the ramparts. The sunshine blazed, the wheat was cut, the valley dry among the vineyards and woods. We were served a perfect summer meal; cold vegetable soup, spinach pie, stuffed zucchinis and berries for dessert, everything cool and light. We ate forever, sat on the terrace and had our *grappa* and *caffè*, watched the swallows zigzag in the sky. Around three thirty they suggested we accompany them to the abandoned monastery of Sant' Anna in Caprenna—where we had once been for a picnic—where they had found an old poet-priest who spoke like no priest they ever heard. He said a late Sunday Mass to a tiny congregation of seven or eight in the ancient church with Sodoma's frescos.

We felt we could survive a short Mass, so we started out toward Pienza, but after a few kilometers turned onto a dirt road heading west in the most silent of valleys. Around the first hill, a *palazzo* beckoned, a blockish three-story structure, long and stately, with beautiful peeling layers of pink stucco.

We dropped through a forest, and ruins peeked out through the trees, and there were deer and peacocks in the shadows. Then we wound past the second *palazzo* with two stately wings and gardens and a lake down below. On went the road through more ruins and a silence broken only by the bells of sheep clanging in the valley. After more twists we were among the cypresses that lead to Sant' Anna. Two cars were parked beside the towering wall, and a small bell was tolling, calling all to Mass. We went in.

The church was enormous and full of shadows, all white, with internal domes, with aged frescoes in the shadows of the apse. There were a dozen pews, but fewer than half a dozen people, and behind a great altar a tall, imposing priest, Don Flori. A full shock of charcoal hair glowed above a giant brow. He was well past seventy, and everything about him—his bulk, his massive hands, his great jaw, and his voice—suggested the majesty of the old volcano on whose slopes he was born and raised. I had never much liked priests, avoided churches except to see their art, but this fellow was captivating. We sat.

Don Flori led his tiny congregation through the rituals but his voice was not of the average priest's toneless, one-key rote, a tired repetition of a thing said a thousand times before. Don Flori's was fresh, full of passion, like a young man's vow. Whatever he said, he meant. Every word. With all his heart.

Then he started the sermon. He came around and stood right before us, before his flock of nine, his great hands holding a paper he didn't read. He bowed his head slightly, gazing at a point between the pews, but his eyes seemed focused on something far beyond. I didn't understand all he said that day, but he talked about time, about passing shadows, about unrecoverable moments, about our humanness. And all the while he spoke, so caring, so concerned, he seemed also to be listening to something, as if he was passing on to us words he was *just then* hearing, words that perhaps came directly from his God.

Then, the Eucharist. He poured the dark-red wine in the silver chalice, placed the hosts on the white linen, dipped each host in the wine and passed it to the three that came to receive, then ate the extra host himself, along with the fallen crumbs. He gulped the wine, wiped the chalice and its rim with the white linen, with great care—holding the linen turning the chalice—then put everything away in the tabernacle, and closed its door.

He said his *"Padre Nostro,"* in all humbleness.

We waited for Don Flori outside under the portico, and he came out in a while, and upon seeing our friends he broke into a big smile. We were introduced. He shook hands with Candace and bade her a firm welcome to Tuscany. Then he turned to me and repeated what he had just been told, "Hungarian born and raised," but with a question. Then he looked straight in my eyes and said mischievously, "Son of Attila, did you come to see Rome or to burn it?"

25 ~ FUNGHI

*A*nd so the summer ended. We had lived six months in Tuscany and felt as if we had never lived in any other place. During the hot weeks Candace painted and I wrote in the cool of the shuttered house, or we wandered in the cool of churches and museums of Florence or Sienna, Perugia, Assisi, Arezzo, or Orvieto—all of them within an hour's drive from the house—or at the seaside near Talamone, cooling off in the green Mediterranean.

Friends from New York and London and Paris drifted in and out, some arriving with ambitious plans to scour all Italy and ending up going no farther than Florence, others like our very dear Patricia from Paris, who wisely announced, "If I don't leave Montepulciano, that's just fine with me."

The rains came in September, hard and dark, pounding the desiccated moonscape of clay, the dust in the road, the ripening grapes, the parched yellowed grass and limp-leafed trees. It splattered on the brick of the *piazzetta* as it came down in curtains, and the air burst to life with a thousand fragrances of lavender, broom, sage and rosemary, as all the plants of the valley breathed again.

Piccardi, looking out our window, gazing at a downpour, whispered with his eyes aglow, *"Funghi."*

Piccardi was an incurable addict. Through his work he traveled much of the countryside, and from the first rain, his eyes were tuned only to *funghi*. He would not hesitate to rise before dawn, drive two hours to the hills of Umbria—where the rains came somewhat sooner—spend the morning crawling on hands and knees through the rain-drenched undergrowth with water trickling down his collar, as silent as he could be so as not to attract other hunters of *funghi*, squinting into the half-light for the mystical *porcini*. When his basket was full, he would cover it with a rag so as not to betray its contents, rush home in his car, and lay them out delicately one by one on the table. He would brush the humus from their stems with delicate, loving strokes, and bask in their view and in his family's awe. God bless him, for what wonderful meals Anna Maria cooked up for us of his hard-earned *funghi*.

The first *funghi*-feast at their house I will never forget. Piccardi casually invited us to taste the year's first finds. It was a Saturday night and we went through graying light, up the hill to their house that looked down on our valley, taking some Vino Nobile and some Pinot Grigio from Orvieto. We had no idea what we would be eating.

The table was set for seven, for their children too were there: feisty Francesca, gentle Angela, and the resolute Alessandro. We chatted about their schooling, about the coming fall, the nearing *vendemmia,* because the grapes might be ready early this year with all the heat. Then the season's first *funghi* appeared, chopped fine, cooked down to a sauce and spread on round *crostini*. It was heaven. The pungent, fragrant *porcini* flavors exploded in our mouths—bittersweet, moody—and the flavors came even more alive with the Vino Nobile from the Avignonesi vineyards.

Having finished the appetizer, I asked if we should open the Pinot Grigio for the next course, but Anna Maria said coyly, "No, there's a bit more *funghi*." That night at the Piccardis' *funghi* rained like manna from heaven. After the *crostini* came *tagliatelle con funghi,* not one but two kinds, the first made with tomatoes, the second with porcini only, cooked with sliced garlic, parsley and salt in oil about twenty minutes, then at the end splashed with wine and simmered for a while. Then came a *zuppa di funghi,* a thick soup of sliced mushrooms, deep, peppery, calling for more wine. After that we were convinced that we had reached the end, leaned back to relax, thanked Anna Maria for a stupendous dinner, when we noticed that Piccardi had been absent for a while. We asked if all was well, and just as Francesca was about to reply, in burst her dad, aproned, grinning, carrying in his arms an enormous plate of grilled *porcini.* Their fragrance wafted across the room and eddied all around us, and their taste made the world's best grilled steak taste dull. We ate. Savoring each bite as if it were our last. The room fell as silent as a tomb.

That was, thank God, the end. Except for some whipped-chocolate cake with a thick sauce of berries, and a bit of *vinsanto,* and coffee, and just a tiny bit of *grappa.*

The next day Candace and I decided that we would go hunt our own *funghi.* She got Bazzotti to weave us a new basket with a hinged lid to help us hide our haul, readied her boots, and cut herself a fine juniper walking stick. We asked Piccardi to please take us with him the next time he went, but for God's sake not before dawn, because rising before dawn is for those going to the gallows.

We asked him to call us when he was going to leave at a more human hour, which he never did. So our first *porcini* hunt was with Paolucci.

He too rose early but only to *governare le bestie*, then to take a turn of the fields, then after a bit of breakfast, we set out at the civilized hour of nine.

Each year mushrooms grow in more or less the same place they have grown before, where the spores fall, and where their mycelium—unless yanked out by a thoughtless gatherer—has been growing for ages. Franco knew the woods around spiral-streeted Petroio like the back of his hand. As a kid he'd played in them, had taken the pigs to root in them, so he knew every nook, every gulch, every hollow, every tree, every shadow of every rock where a *porcino* might grow. We took our virgin basket and set out.

We followed a tractor trail into the woods, walking or crawling and sometimes waddling like hunchback ducks under dense woods that grew and crisscrossed like cobwebs near the ground. Paolucci went at full speed, sweeping with a single gaze a patch of underbrush, then finding or not finding *porcini* or *lecciaioli*, he moved, like a quick spider, in unforeseen directions. We tried our best to follow him, but it took us only minutes to become separated and lost. We called to Paolucci, to each other, until finally, impatiently, Paolucci gave a sign, and then we hurried toward where his voice had been. When we got there he was gone. But at least Candace and I were together. Candace screamed, "Lookout! *Porcini!*" But it was too late. She stared in disgust and sorrow at my feet. I had found my first *porcino*: big, fresh, beautiful, and mulched to a pulp under my foot.

Well, at least I had the knack. All I had to do was watch my step. I waddled slowly on, one tree at a time, with my face almost to the ground. At last I found one. Candace looked at me with unguarded admiration. My pride swelled. I waddled on. The undergrowth ripped off my hat, clutched my sleeves, slapped my face, but I found another. Then another. I was delirious. Candace found one too and she told me to stay put until she came and cut the stems with the Swiss Army knife to let the spores remain for next year, for the next fool.

Paolucci erupted from the scrub, his shirttail pouched, and full of porcini. Within an hour our basket was full. We were scratched and out of breath and our backs ached from being bent in two, but a joy like that could never be equaled. We hurried back to the car and home to Nonna to show her the fruits of our labor. She glanced at the basketful of mushrooms, then, not given to wild emotions, looked approvingly and said, "*Buon lavoro*." Good work.

The fire was aglow with coals. We cleaned the mushrooms, removed the stems—those would be used for sauce along with broken caps—took the best caps we could find, gingerly removed the leaves and dirt, poured on some olive oil and ground on a bit of salt, then slipped them gently on a grill over the coals. We turned them once or twice, adding a bit of oil to help them brown, then laid them on big plates. With a little bread, a light salad and red wine we had, without exaggeration, the feast of our lives—gathered with our own hands.

Nothing in the world tastes as good.

26 ~ VENDEMMIA

We looked forward to our first *vendemmia* like children look forward to Christmas. Old Italian movies flashed before our eyes; the young picking grapes, brawny laughing men hauling grapes in *bigonzi* strapped over their shoulders, barefooted women stomping grapes in great vats, the must running, and at day's end the great meal—the long table under the arbor, laden with food and wine, surrounded by happy, boisterous people.

Halfway through September the grapes had fully blushed, looking as dark as they could possibly get. When Paolucci and I sampled his most southerly vineyard, the grapes tasted flavorful and sweet to me, but he crushed a grape between his fingers, rubbed away the juice, then touched them against each other and said, "Not enough sugar yet. My fingers don't stick." So the date for the *vendemmia* was set for the first weekend in October.

We rose early. The low autumn sun slanted across the hills, ground fog still huddled below us in the valley, and the crisp air against our faces told us that summer was over. High on the ridge,

Paolucci's old orange tractor swung out of his yard, pulling the battered metal cart, and behind him in a straggling line, already talking at the top of their voices, directing, arguing, advising, bantering, was the *vendemmia* party, of the entire Paolucci family plus inlaws. There was Franco's sister Anna, big voice, round face, either admonishing or laughing; and her husband, rotund Pasquino, who loved all women madly; and Rosanna's dad, gaunt with a constant cigarette; and Rosanna's quiet brother; and noisy Bazzotti.

The tractor slowed and the crowd bunched up on the ridge and argued about where to begin. It was astounding that with only three small vineyards, everyone had thought of a different place— high, low, flat or hill, shade or sun, this end or that—and they all talked at once. Then Candace said quietly but firmly that we better get started because I think it's going to rain. "How can it rain from a clear blue sky?" Bazzotti shrilled, and Nonna mumbled glaring at him, *"Più ignorante d'una gallina,"* Dumber than a hen, and Pasquino laughed in utter approval, and scratched himself joyfully between his legs.

Then we began. Each of us took a *paniere*, the shape of basket Little Red Riding Hood carried to Grandma's house, and we fanned out along two rows of vines, some of us on one side and some on the other, and finally the *vendemmia* began.

The clusters of grapes were enormous and dense, peeking out from under fading leaves. I groped around for the stem of one near me, found it, and pulled. Nothing happened. I pulled again. The vine shook. Then I noticed Nonna standing beside me, holding out a pair of pruning shears, smiling kindly and saying, *"Sono più forte di noi."* They're stronger than us. It was only then that I heard the subtle clicking of everyone's pruning sheers as they clipped the thick, woody stems of the grapes.

Paolucci swung his tractor and cart between the narrow rows and everyone scrambled for his life. Once past us, he switched off the motor, clambered back into his cart and stood among the pile of tall containers, the *bigonzi,* which yawned empty awaiting the grapes. We snipped and cut and chatted away, kidding, bantering, yelling and laughing—just like the movies—calling for someone to come and take away the loaded *panieri* and bring empty ones—*Madonna benedetta*—because where can we put the grapes, in our pockets? And Pasquino, waiting for his basket, dangled an enormous compact clump of grapes before his pants and called to his wife Anna, "What does this remind you of?"

She laughed loudly and shook her head. "Your dreams."

The vineyard rang with laughter.

We lugged the full baskets to the cart and hoisted them up to Paolucci, who emptied them into the *bigonzi* scraping the last crushed grapes from the bottom with his fingers. The sticky nectar was dripping everywhere. It ran down our hands, it ran down our shears, and ran down the baskets and into our shoes. Bees buzzed. The wind rose; the sky to the south had darkened with clouds. By mid-morning the *bigonzi* were full and tightly packed against each other, and we lashed them all together with a rope. The tractor lurched and we followed it up to the *cantina.*

Paolucci backed the tractor under the old roof that covered the brick *forno* and the *cantina* door, and we lifted the beastly heavy *bigonzi* to the ground. Then we crushed. We didn't crush with our feet, but used great carved wooden pestles. The grapes turned to must—unfermented wine. Then, to reduce the weight, we poured half of the must into an empty *bigonzo,* lugged the now half-full ones inside, and shoved them up the old wooden ladder to Paolucci with cries of Oh my back, Oh my God, Oh my hernia, and How can you have a hernia when you have no balls? Then we poured the crushed grapes into the vats.

When the cart and the *bigonzi* were all empty, we headed back to the vineyard again. The black clouds had edged nearer and a cold breeze blew that smelled and felt of rain.

"What do you say now, *Meteorologo?*" Pasquino joshed Bazzotti.

"Not a drop of rain," Bazzotti snapped.

"At least hens lay eggs," Nonna said.

We began picking again. What a great satisfaction to pick those grapes, great bursting clusters, many of which weighed well over a kilo—a whole bottle of wine right there in my hands. Time seemed to slow, and I was reminded of simpler days centuries past. It was a labor that bound us to ancient tradition and to each other, if only for a moment.

As we neared noon, the wind brought the fragrance of roast meat and garlic, and onions stewing, from the direction of the house. We accelerated the pace like horses that smelled the stable. We felt the weights of the *bigonzi* less as we wrestled them up the ladder, just rushed those last loads, then went into the house to eat. The church bells tolled midday. Dark clouds were sweeping toward San Biagio.

We feasted. Loudly. The bottles of wine seldom stopping, and no one noticing that outside, the day had turned to night, until the dreaded sound of hail clattered on the windows. Everyone fell silent. The forks stopped, faces turned weary. A minute of pounding could turn the grapes to mush and they could mildew within hours. We went to the door and windows. The hail sputtered then stopped, but the day was darker than twilight. Across the valley a great gray curtain obscured the hill and town.

"Cannetto's getting *martellato*," Paolucci said. Hammered.

"What do they care," Il Suocero said, "they have hail insurance;"

"And you don't?" Candace asked.

"Ha. Us?" Rosanna said.

"We better go then," Candace said. "I think it's going to rain."

And even Bazzotti laughed in grudging admiration.

We picked like ones possessed. The shears flashed and Paolucci loaded like a demon. Across the valley you could hear the hail hiss, riddling the air. We threw grapes, we threw *panieri*, we ran from vine to vine, and the cart was almost loaded when the sky fell upon us. Rain. We threw a tarp over the *bigonzi* to stop the rain from watering down the wine, put the *panieri* over our heads, and ran for the protection of the *cantina*. We huddled with the chickens and the pigeons and watched the rain make rivers in the barnyard.

The rain moved quickly on. A hard wind whipped the black clouds past the towers of the town. The wind blew through the night and dried the vines. In the morning, under a bright sun, we loaded up and waded out for the second day of the *vendemmia*, slipping and sinking in the mud. New reinforcements came, Carla's husband-to-be, and some cousins from out of town, and we picked and griped about the mud.

That night after the last *bigonzo* was poured into the vat, and all the baskets and *bigonzi* were washed and rinsed and turned upside down to dry, and the mud was hosed from the cart and our boots, we sat down in the long entry hall with all the tables end to end. We ate and laughed and drank—just like in the movies—stuffed ourselves with *crostini,* and then the pastas—*gnocchi,* potato dumplings with mushrooms and *pici* with chicken liver—then stuffed veal, and stewed tripe, and all kinds of roast birds and pork and rabbit, and Anna's specialty, snails—that she gathered in some secret woods—cooked in tomatoes, garlic, oil, and a bit of wine, and roast potatoes and finely chopped salad drenched in olive oil, then cheeses and then so many *dolci* that I couldn't count them all, with sparkling wine and *vinsanto,* until Pasquino, in his leather cap, leaned back against the wall, put his head down on his chest and began an uproarious, window-rattling snore. Bazzotti was so drunk he slurred; I was so drunk I spoke flawless Italian; and Paolucci was so drunk he went and got more wine.

That was our first *vendemmia.*

God bless the grape.

~

At the Thursday market gathering of the men from the countryside, rumor had it that Nebbia had found a load of new old things the week before. Early that evening we went to see. We drove through the hills near sunset; the vines had all turned yellow, the wheat fields were all plowed, the autumn silence reigned in the countryside before November's seeding and December's olive picking.

We looked for him at his house, his shed, the *piazza,* the bar and finally found him at the town's low-ceilinged social club, playing cards, blowing smoke rings in the air. He greeted us with an *"Oh, chi si vede!"* Who does one see? and rose instantly, fought his way through the smoke, and taking Candace by the arm, escorted us out into the fresh, crisp, autumn air. We chatted and walked through town and down the road to his shed, and up the long stone steps to his room of ancient ware. There was a wonderful small cherry-wood trunk that we instantly bought, along with a tiny but heavy oak bench that seemed to have been made for the strongest of the Seven Dwarfs.

Nebbia, in his chair, lamented lengthily how there was nothing worth gathering left in Tuscany, and how he was thinking of closing up his shed and beginning a new life with his dog in the noble occupation of hunting for truffles.

At the sound of the word truffles my teeth clenched. Candace's face lit up. Nebbia was thrilled. "You like truffles?" he beamed.

"I'd kill for them," she said.

Nebbia was on his feet. "*Andiamo*," he said, and virtually pushed us out the door. "The friend who is teaching my dog to hunt for truffles has already found some. White truffles. The best. He sells them at murderous prices to restaurants, so he hates to sell at human prices to his neighbors, but don't worry."

We went up the road to find Giovanni the truffle king, and without knocking opened the door and called out "*Permesso*" and landed in a kitchen where a young family was getting ready for dinner. Giovanni flinched. But he begged us to sit down anyway and have a glass of wine, and we accepted and chatted about truffles, why they grow under poplars and walnuts but don't like it under pines. Then Nebbia blurted out that we'd like to buy a little.

"I don't have much," Giovanni protested.

"They don't want much," Nebbia said.

"I have little."

"They want little."

"Anything," Candace pleaded like an addict.

"*Preciso*," Nebbia said.

Giovanni sat and stared then, realizing that his nightmare wasn't going away, he got up, locked the front door with a key, dragged himself into a little room and came back with a bundled kerchief in his hand. He put it on the table well out of our reach, unwrapped it, pulled out a brown paper bundle, unwrapped that, pulled out a tiny paper bag, opened it and poured its contents onto the open kerchief. I felt as if we were doing some big drug deal, but then outpoured a dozen grayish lumps the size of cherries and a pungent violent smell, almost acrid, filled the air. A sad joy glowed on Giovanni's face. He handled the lumps as if they were diamonds, sliding them over to us one by one, and we had three in front of us, and Candace reached to touch one when something like a head banged hard against the door and swore at creative length. Giovanni leapt. He swept up his jewels and shouted "*Arrivo,*" but ran into the little room instead and slammed a drawer then slammed the door. He grabbed the cigarette out of Nebbia's mouth, took a bunch of violent puffs and belched the smoke all around us. Then he called out in a voice so fakely calm that all of us started laughing, "*Arrivo! Dio Santo.*" And he went.

In came a confused well-dressed neighbor, "*Buona sera, buona sera.*" He sat and chatted about all sorts of nonsense, then finally he blurted out that he heard Giovanni had found some white truffles and he'd like to buy a piece. Giovanni plain faced lied that he hadn't found a one.

"It's true," Nebbia concurred. "He's useless."

When the neighbor left, we settled on about ten dollars, then we too left with Nebbia. "He's still very upset," Nebbia said outside. "Two weeks ago his family came from the mountains for a visit, his grandmother too, and she got up early in the morning, and decided to make a big breakfast for them all. She looked for ingredients in the fridge, found eggs, then she found some truffles, a hefty bag, scrambled the eggs, then wanting to be a good grandma, sliced the truffles on top, thick slices, all of them, about five-hundred dollars worth if sold to restaurants, then she called everyone to the table because she had a surprise. Giovanni couldn't speak for three days."

We drove home, and I swore to Candace the truffles were poisoned because I had never smelled anything so violent in my life, like poison gas, and she finally said fine and held the truffles out the window and also said that if she dropped one I would not get home alive.

At home the truffles stank up the whole house. We put them outside on the widow ledge between the window and the shutters because I was sure the gas would kill us by morning.

We had truffles with everything imaginable for a week. Candace even made a mozzarella and truffles sandwich. I guess you could call divine monotony the essence of Tuscany.

27 ~ VENICE NIGHTS

*I*nevitably my birthday rolled around. Candace and I had always forgone wrapped-up birthday presents and chose instead to take a trip around those special days. We had done well over the years, from the Seychelles to Norway, Japan to Tibet, but the most unforgettable one was years ago, in the heart of Costa Rica.

We were in the capital, San Jose, a city of old Spanish architecture. On the map, to the east, a roadless wilderness lumbered to the Caribbean. Through it a thin, black line—a railroad—twisted its way to the port of Limon. Six hours on a train. After months of living in a Volkswagen camper, what a luxury: lunch in the dining car, a few nights in a quaint beach hotel, dinners in small fish restaurants. Paradise.

We packed for a few days, went down to the station, bought tickets, sat and waited for the train. It was a small station, and I thought it was charming how they dedicated a part of it for a train museum, for across from us on the last of two tracks were three ancient, tiny, narrow, wooden railroad cars in museum condition, painted brilliant red. The astoundingly narrow-gauge track, the tiny wheels, the shortness of its cars made it look like a thing out of a theme park. People got on it and sat by the open windows. We thought they wanted to get a feel of olden times. An antique engine huffed and puffed into the station, banged hard into the three little cars jostling the people, coupled on, and without further fussing, began to pull out. Heading east. We scrambled aboard. Our fellow passengers smiled.

The railroad cars were wooden boxes with two rows of two-seat, wood-slat benches. No luggage racks, no footrests, no headrests, no trimmings. And no dining car. On the entire train not a bite to eat. Except in the lap of the big man across from us, who from a paper bag pulled an interminable supply of ugly small bananas and stuffed them in his mouth. He finally offered us some. They were delicious. The little train grew on you after a while.

We were in tropical jungle-covered hills; enormous vegetation heaved in languid waves with the passing of the train. Then suddenly half the world dropped away. Where the jungle had seemed impenetrable just a moment before, there was only air. And when you stuck your head out the window and looked down, you recoiled in panic, because a step from the track, the world was an abyss.

"Five thousand Chinamen die," our big friend said gently. "Building train. Fall down. Long way. Nobody see again."

He told us, half in English, half in Spanish, about the horrors of etching this little steel line onto the enormous jungle cliff; how it took ten years to lay barely twenty miles; how the Chinese workers tied themselves to trees at night to sleep, and how the mud slides swept them away anyway, trees and all.

Then we pulled into a tiny station and were attacked. *"Papà! Papà! Papà!"* barefoot urchins cried climbing in through doors and windows, dragging loaded, plastic garbage bags behind them. They stopped before us gasping *"papà, papà,"* and pulled from their bags hot, fresh French fries and steaming cobs of corn. Everyone bought and everyone ate. Then we pulled back out into the bush again.

There were wood shacks on stilts in the jungle without roads, with huge trays full of coffee beans and cocoa beans drying in the sun, and barefoot kids waving at the train. And the closer we got to the Caribbean the more African the faces became, and big signs at the ramshackle stations shouted, "Chills? Fever? It *mihgt* be malaria!" And then the sky went black. It began to rain. A downpour. As if the train were running under a waterfall. The wind brought the rain inside so I got up to close the windows. But there were no windows. Only holes. Everyone huddled on the dry ends of the benches.

Night fell. I got up to turn on the lights. But there were no lights. I searched around with a flickering lighter, but there were no sockets, no wires, no switches. The rain poured in an impenetrable dark. With the roar of the air, and the train, and the rain, you had to yell to be heard. So we sat silent in the thunder. We went on.

The station at Limon wasn't much brighter than the darkness. And it poured. We asked for a good hotel. The man smiled; there was only one hotel. Period. We ran through curtains of rain in the mud-streets jumping puddles. The clapboard town looked like a Western movie except that every rain-drenched sign on every rain-drenched shop was in Chinese. The hotel was a tall shack. Up a dim stairway, the large landing was the innkeeper's living room. She sat in a chair listening to a radio, and beside her on a little table was her old skinny dog. Stuffed. The room had French doors but the panes of glass were missing. There was no mattress. There was a great bag stuffed with straw like a sleeping elephant. We napped with our clothes on, and our shoes. We went to eat in the only place in town, basic bare and no-nonsense, but the best Chinese food I ever ate.

The morning was humid over the Caribbean. That was my twenty-sixth birthday.

So sixteen years later to the day, we took a train to Venice. There were padded seats and little tables, and windows and window shades and a dining car with linen and silverware. But I missed the *papàs* and the darkness.

The air is opaque and full of molten colors when Vaporetto #2 bumps against the scow. The deckhand throws the bow line on the bollard, wraps the bitter end on the twin-horned cleat aboard, and the pilot holds the *vaporetto* tight against the barge with the force of the engine. The rope cries. The scow rocks from the wake, and people shuffle off and we shuffle on. We always sit on the aft deck looking aft, then we can pretend we're on the boat alone.

It is twilight and the air is misty, and you know the fog is rising out on the lagoon. The light is silver-pink, like vaporized pearls. We glide, and the wakes spread onto the seaweed-covered stones of the Scuola dei Morti, which is the Confraternity of the Dead, and I'd rather not know exactly what that refers to. We glide past a gawky church, and the fog is already oozing down the Canale di Cannaregio. The tide is ebbing. The air, thick with iodine, smells like the bottom of the sea. Lights go on in windows down the narrow Rios, and light up the fog as candles light angel hair. We wrap our scarves around our faces and hug on the aft deck.

Ponte di Rialto rises from a diffuse and fluttering light. Twelve arches with the master touch of a larger arch instead of a keystone: what arrogance, what grace. At Rialto the *vaporetto* makes mass passenger changes. A girl comes to the aft deck, pretty, short-cropped hair, serious face, carrying a paper bag of clementines. She begins to peel one, but first decides to wrap her shawl tighter, and puts the clementine down on the rail. We lurch. The clementine falls, splashes then bobs, a violent orange on the gray silk of the waves. She smiles a shy, wise smile and you wonder if she's not in from the country.

We're coming to the end of the canal, the grand finale: first Palazzo Dario, small, but its facade provocatively unbalanced, then the majestically lacy Santa Maria della Salute with her brood of domes, and finally that graceful figure, so light on one foot, atop the giant golden globe of the customs house. Here too the fog is rising. At Santa Maria del Giglio we get off. The clementine-eater smiles good-bye. We walk to our small hotel at the end of the narrow alley and the concierge laughs, "You two of little luggage. *Ben tornati*," and gives us the room we ask for overlooking the immaculate garden of a *palazzo* and its great hall of a *soggiorno*, with its chandelier like a haystack, and furniture that would make a museum proud. And over its roof, the domes and lantern of Santa Maria della Salute with the big saint on the top, all so ethereal in the pearly light you're not sure if its there or just a memory. We throw open both windows. The foghorn bellows on the darkening lagoon.

Our friend and fellow sailor Emilio, who owns one of the finest restaurants in Venice, has invited us for dinner to his *palazzo*. It's on a small canal in the most quiet part of Venice, and we'll never find it with all the twists, turns, dead ends and bridges, so he tells us to meet him at eight on Ponte della Academia, the only bridge south of the Rialto to cross the Grand Canal.

We bundle up and head out in the fog. We wander down dark, alley-wide streets, and over the angled, tiny, high-arched bridges, up stairs, through *piazzas* and up the wood steps of the Accademia. We're early. We lean on the railing and stare at the Grand Canal and its flickering lights, and we squint and pretend they're all torches and wax candles, and messages can only be carried by furtive caped figures or whispered excitedly in passing, and anything can happen to anyone in the fog. Perhaps that is still a great draw of Venice—the potential mystery. And potential romance. That could start so simply, with a fallen clementine bobbing on the waves.

"Lost dinner guests, I presume," Emilio says softly beside us. Big smiles and greetings.

His house is as unpredictable as Venice itself: twisting, inside-outside stairways, half-lit landings, rooftop terraces, magnificently indulgent Venetian chimneys, and the waters of a canal lapping at its feet. The seafood dinner Emilio and his wife Anna prepare we use as a gastronomic measuring stick for years. The appetizers of mushrooms and fishes *sottolio*, the *spaghetti alle vongole*, the grilled *dentice* and *orate* with a parsley sauce, and the desserts and wines are all delicate and *giusto,* just right. And we talk about the wonders of Venice and the wonders of Tuscany and the joys of sailing, and we settle that in the spring we will sail his wooden sloop across the lagoon to Piazza San Marco, like voyagers arriving centuries ago.

We leave well after midnight, heads aswim with the last

champagne, and we ease out of the courtyard into the narrow alley into a city that has vanished in the fog. We cross one little bridge, and another, and another and turn left under an archway, which I wisely noted on our arrival to use as a landmark on our return, and we cross a *piazzetta*, and another bridge and then we are absolutely and irretrievably lost, after midnight, in the fog. There is no movement and no sound, only the foghorn somewhere on the far side of the world. We move slowly, uncertainly, turning when the streets end in canals. We keep along a sizable canal with fog-drenched boats tied to shore, but the walkway dead-ends at a small canal, and walls of houses stand in the murky water. A bell tolls one. We turn back. We stumble upon a *piazzetta* with marble paving and search for signs on the walls, but the walls are blank layers of crumbling stucco. We make suggestions, study bridges, listen for the muffled foghorn, listen for a *vaporetto* that might give us a hint as to the Grand Canal, but there is nothing. Only soft, indistinguishable sounds in the fog now and then. We are as thrilled as kids on Christmas Eve. When we find a big *piazza* with trees we recognize, we feel almost disappointed, but cheer up when after two turns we're lost again. Finally a soul. A tired lady sweeping out a cafe with its chairs up on the tables gives us two hot chocolates out of sheer Christian mercy. And such clear directions that it will be impossible for us to get lost again. But we manage. We find what we think is the Grand Canal, twice, but both times at dead ends, and we turn back baffled into the labyrinth of fog. We begin to know every canal, every alley, every bridge, every house. Everything but the way out. A bell tolls, muffled in the fog.

It is two o'clock and the fog absolute when we stumble onto Rialto Bridge. In its great arch full of misty light, Candace, flushed from the wine and the cold, looks up with mischievous eyes. "Next time you get lost, promise to take me with you."

I promise.

"Happy birthday, Chum."

28 ~ WOODCUTTING

A languid warmth and the colors of autumn lingered on and on. Long after the vines turned and the poplars lost their leaves, the oaks and pomegranates paled at their leisure. Sometime after the *vendemmia*, we laid aside our watches. It was easy to tell time by the late sunrise and early sunset, and the morning, noon and evening tolling of the bells. There were other gentle markers of the day: the sound of the mailman's little Fiat on the gravel, Bazzotti's dogs barking as he fed them upon coming home from town, and when the wind was right, the glee of the children dashing into the yard for recess at the monastery of the nuns. Near that same time, I don't recall when or why, we decided that while the bells tolled we would stop whatever toil, and give our backs and minds a rest, and gaze at the beauty around us: the hills, town, clouds, the light, or a falcon drifting on the rising air.

Suddenly one morning we awoke to winter. Cold air had slipped down from the north during the night and turned the warm sea air that had been there into a fog so thick it hid even the hedge. The church bells tolled dull and distant like old memories.

The north wind, the *tramontana,* blew the fog away, and it grew colder and colder with every passing hour, until you could no longer work in the open fields. The Paoluccis took refuge in the shelter of the woods and began cutting firewood for the winter. The winding stream had a rambling woods along it, widest where the bull had died, narrower where we forded below the towered ruin, and this year they decided to thin the woods there.

In Tuscany one does not cut trees—not even one's own— without the forester's permission. Each little woods is carefully marked on the region's maps, and is not to be reduced in area for any reason, although once every twelve years one can thin the stands. Thinning means leaving a tree standing about every five meters, so that after thinning the woods still look like woods, but clean and well groomed like a park. This strict law has helped keep Tuscany beautiful to this day, with tiny woods among the fields, and along streams and gullies, and on hillsides too steep to plow.

The Paoluccis had been cutting wood for a day when I joined them. I took a shortcut across the hay fields one morning, then homed in on the curl of smoke rising from below. Nonna too had come to help that day, and the three of them were cutting out dead wood; dried oaks and poplars lay on the ground. Franco worked the chainsaw, first limbing the fallen giants and then cutting up the trunks, while Rosanna with a *penatta,* a short, fat, curved machete, lobbed off twigs and smaller branches. Nonna gathered the better twigs and tied them into bundles, and the rest she threw onto the blazing fire. I hauled the rounds—the biggest ones with Nonna's help—and loaded them neat and tight onto the cart.

By the time the noon bell tolled we had half a load stacked, and the fire had burned down to a mountain of ashes, its center a heap of glowing coals. We were a long walk from home, and a long ride on the slow tractor, so we had our lunches there. I had brought some cheese and cold meats, but Rosanna smiled and said keep those for later, because when you work in the woods you need a good hot lunch to give you strength.

She poked about in the pile of ashes and pulled out a small covered pot that steamed under the lid, and a wonderful fragrance of cooked onions filled the air. Nonna brought a wooden fruit-box from the tractor, and from it out came plates, forks, bread, wine, and tin cups, and a brown paper full of veal chops. We sat on rounds of wood around the coals and Rosanna dished a steaming sauce onto the plates. Long transparent strips swam in olive oil red from tomatoes and paprika, and I broke a chunk of bread and poured myself a cup of wine. I ate and ate and loved it, but could not for the life of me figure out what it was. Rosanna laughed and said, "*Cipolle*," onions. I have never tasted anything better. Then she grilled the veal chops on the fire, and we wolfed them down and wiped our plates with chunks of bread. Then I lay back on a bed of logs to give my aching bones a rest and watched the branches sway against the sky.

After lunch those rounds of logs flew onto the cart. Near dusk, we roped the big pile down and followed the tractor homeward. Once out of the woods, the wind hit and we bundled up and quickened our pace, and by the time we climbed the hill to the first ruin we were warm again. I could see the light of home glowing in the distance.

29 ~ PORCA

*T*he hoar frost set one morning and the valley sparkled white as if under a breath of snow. When the sun rose, the world glittered, and specks of light were refracted through the melting beads. The countryside was still. It was too soon to pick olives, too soon to prune vines, too late to seed wheat or oats, too late and too cold for *funghi*.

Our woodpile was high. In the outbuilding, onions and garlic hung braided, potatoes were spread on a layer of cane, and apples—tiny and blemished but so full of flavor—glowed red on a bed of straw over an old door on sawhorses. Clusters of white grapes hung from a pole away from the wall, to dry and slowly turn into sweet raisins. Our young walnut grove had yielded three baskets of walnuts, small and dark, and these we laid in a fraying basket near the door to give them lots of air.

We had bought two demijohns of wine—one from Paolucci and one from Crociani, up the hill—and with great fanfare got ready to siphon it off into bottles. We bought a hundred new bottles from the *consorzio agrario*, the farm store, along with a treasure of a corker, a wonderful levered contraption that miraculously squeezes the cork while a big pin on the lever presses it home. We siphoned and filled, and topped off and spilled and lost the siphon and had to siphon again. Halfway through I was cross-eyed and had to go out for air. But by nightfall the bottles were full and corked and we stuck little labels on them, and scribbled on the name and year, then laid the bottles up in the little cellar on wooden shelves I had made out of rough planks. A heartwarming sight.

Our favorite butcher had given us a good price on a whole hind-leg of *prosciutto,* nice and lean, and *stagionata*, aged hard and dry, because it was from last winter's kill. The hardness was disliked by the locals—lucky for us because the older the *prosciutto* the richer its flavor, and if it's a bit chewy, well, it's worth the extra work. So with the whole leg under my arm I walked proudly through town, and hung it from a wire in the middle of the cellar, with a holed tin plate over it to keep off adventurous mice.

We were ready for winter.

By midmorning the frost had melted everywhere except in the hollows, and I went out to split some kindling. I had worked up a good sweat when I heard a clop, clop, clopping on the road behind me. It was Franco, smiling, bouncing down the road, riding bareback on a small, fat pony he had bought the week before. His feet dangled, almost touching ground, and he was having the time of his life, looking every bit like Sancho Panza, but with a piece of bread and sausage in his hand.

"*Che ne pensi?*" he called with his mouth full. What do you think of it?

"*Stupendo*," I said. "You look just like John Wayne. I'm jealous."

"Why don't you get one too," he said. "We can ride together."

"Tomorrow," I said.

"Not tomorrow," he countered. "Tomorrow we kill a pig."

The hoar frost was back the next morning, thick and white and the air even crisper. I had forgotten about the pig. I was sitting in the kitchen by the fire, still in my bathrobe, sipping a cappuccino and stumbling through an old Italian paper, when the pig squealed. The sound echoed through the valley. I dressed and went alone, Candace telling me to call her when the sausages were ready. I had passed the pond when the pig charged across the road trailing a rope around its neck, and ran into the hay shed, sending up a cloud of chickens. Pasquino in a butcher's apron and Paolucci in rubber boots ran close behind. They came back onto the road, Franco leading the pig, tugging the rope, and Pasquino walking beside him. Back in the yard Franco stopped, and Pasquino for a better grip took the loop of the rope and straddled the pig. The pig bolted, squealing. And Pasquino, half running, half riding, bounced and skipped on top of it, swearing at the top of his lungs. The pig rodeo was on. Anna slowed the pig by blocking its way with a shovel, but Nonna, standing beside the steaming cauldron where water was boiling for the kill, took her old broom and gave the pig a resounding swat across the ass to speed it up again. Pasquino roared and the pig squealed and Anna laughed louder than the two of them together. Bazzotti appeared from nowhere and shrilled instructions to everyone but no one gave a damn and Paolucci, philosophically, lit a cigarette. Then the pig, tiring, ran into a corner and Pasquino held on, cursing, and then I heard the shot. It was soft and muffled but the pig went down like deadwood, with a very tidy hole just above his eyes.

"*Porca*," Pasquino said. Swine.

Then they gave the pig a proper bath and shave.

We dragged it onto a wooden pallet to keep it out of the mud that was to come, then Nonna poured buckets of boiling water over it, and Anna scrubbed it with a brush. Pasquino pulled out an old barber's razor and a strap, hung it from a rusty nail in the stable door, slapped the razor over it, then, humming a little tune, knelt down and began to shave the pig. He started from the shoulders back, long smooth strokes, and ended up with small, careful, tidy ones around the ears. Humming. Nonna kept pouring the boiling, steaming water. When the pig was squeaky clean, pink and hairless, we flipped it over onto a wooden ladder, laid it on its back, tied its hind piggy feet above the topmost rung, then wrestled the beast-loaded ladder and leaned it up against the wall. Then Pasquino went to sharpen his set of knives—tough, thick-bladed things he had made, with beautiful olivewood handles—and I walked back home to get my rubber boots. The smell of wood smoke drifted down the road.

When I returned, the pig was already opened wide, all cleaned out, and Nonna now poured hot water inside it for the last rinse. Anna was in the small room next to the stable, cutting up fat to boil in a big pot on a wood-burning stove, and Rosanna was scrubbing the guts then dipping them in boiling water to be used as skin for sausages. Pasquino hummed and butchered, changing strokes, changing knives, and Paolucci, like a first-class host, smoked a cigarette and drank wine, while everyone sent him on short errands.

All day the dressing and preparing went on: sausages, headcheese, salamis, the four *prosciutti*—all fat carved away, trimmed and rounded—and chops, and long ribs to be grilled on the fire, and that most sought-after piece, the *lombo*, the delicate filet along the spine. We paused only for lunch, a quick affair with stewed tripe and fresh scrumpet, the crunchy, tasty bits that remain after the fat had been cooked down then pressed. Then back to the warm little room beside the stable.

Anna and Rosanna prepared *fegatelli*—cooked liver cut into plum-size pieces, netted and put under oil for winter. I lugged the four, washed, rewashed and towel-dried hams—the *prosciutti*—one by one, up into the cool and drafty attic, laid them on a reed-covered table, and waited for Nonna to come up and prepare them. She came slowly with a small sack, followed by Franco carrying a pot. She rested, then began. First she worked from the pot of cooled vinegar that had boiled with garlic, rosemary sprigs, pepper-corns, and some *pepperoncini*—tiny, viciously hot peppers. She bathed each ham slowly, then laid them with the skin down on the cane, and began to salt them. She scooped mounds of salt from the cloth bag and spread it, leaving a thick white layer like fresh snow. For the next twenty-five days she would return every morning to touch up areas that have soaked through, and to lay on just a sprin-kling more of salt. On the twenty-fifth day she would scrub off all the salt, and apply a coat of ground black pepper. The next day they were hung and would remain undisturbed for at least two months. Then they were ready to be sliced thin with a knife and savored. How the hell anyone can sit there and stare at that thing for two months without devouring it is truly beyond me.

It was getting dark and biting cold by the time the cleaning up was done. We carried the *lombo*, salamis, and strings of sausages into the kitchen and hung them to dry from the beams, like festive bunting. Then Rosanna put some fresh chops and ribs and sausages to grill, and as their fragrance filled the air, lo and behold there is Candace at the door saying, "Are the sausages ready?" and coming in with a big tart of sliced apples and wild-plum jam.

We began to eat. Pasquino, who eats and drinks well at the best of times, was in particularly strong form.

"You're eating like Bricco," Anna said.

"No one eats like Bricco," Paolucci said. And Pasquino wanted to answer but his mouth was too full for breathing, so he nodded.

"Bricco could eat a house," Paolucci said.

"And the land from under it," Nonna said.

"Who is Bricco?" I asked.

"Bricco is a huge guy from Montisi who drives a truck."

"But mostly eats," Rosanna said.

"And drinks," Anna retorted. "One night at a *festa* in Pienza he drank seventy glasses of wine."

"Or seven hundred," Paolucci said.

"What seven hundred!?" Rosanna said.

Paolucci waved away the detail with his hand. "Bricco is as big as any cow," Paolucci said. "For his morning snack in his truck, he puts a kilo loaf of bread under an arm, a two-liter bottle of wine between his legs, a whole string of sausage, like you see hanging on the beam, around his neck, then takes a bite of bread, bite of sausage, long drink of wine. Meanwhile he drives."

"Or eel," Pasquino said, coming up for air. "Takes a long loaf of bread, rips it open lengthwise, sticks in a whole cooked eel, longer than my . . ."

"Don't start!!" Anna yelled.

". . . longer than a rolling pin, takes a whole salted cod, grabs it by the tail, knocks the *puttana* against a stone wall a few times, bang, bang to knock off the salt, throws it in the loaf to keep the eel company, and he's ready for lunch."

"And drinks like ten of us," Paolucci said. "At Pienza after he drank those seven hundred glasses . . ."

"What seven hundred!?" Rosanna yelled.

"What difference does it make? *Madonna Serpente!*" Paolucci roared. "He drinks, he drinks, *punto!* Anyway there he is at Pienza, three o'clock in the morning, and I see him crawling around his truck, reaching over his head now and then feeling the tires, the bumper, the hood, the sides. What's the matter, Bricco, I says, don't you feel well? I feel perfect, he says grinning. But I can't find the door. Fifteen years I've driven this truck and now I can't find the *cazzo* door. You're too drunk to drive home anyway, I says. Who needs to drive? he says. Just help me find the door and get in; the damned truck knows the way. And he never had an accident in his life."

"And polite," Pasquino said. "When he saw some old lady, he'd stop that great truck of his, get out and carry her bags and help her across the street."

"Bricco di Montisi," Paolucci said.

"Seven hundred glasses of wine in one night," Rosanna said.

And we laughed and ate and drank, laughed over Bricco and over Pasquino's wild pig ride, ate and drank until Pasquino, in his leather cap, leaned back against the wall, let his head fall on his chest and began his traditional, window-rattling snore.

30 ~ SNOW

A ferocious *tramontana* blasted from the north for two long days in December. It whipped the cypresses into respectful bows, tore off the last leaves, flattened the reeds, whistled through every crevice in the house, blew all the chickens' feathers in the wrong direction and made them huddle with the ducks and cats and dogs on the leeward side of houses. It blew cold and mean, blew in the light, blew in the dark, blew while we ate, blew while we slept, blew while we tried to talk or think. At night it rattled whatever it could find: doors, windows, shutters, gutters, nerves. It imprisoned us. We longed for the town but knew its narrow streets were now wind tunnels, so we stoked the fire and stayed put. Nothing moved in the countryside unless moved by the wind. Then the wind ran off to somewhere in Africa but the cold stayed.

The next morning we felt reborn. A calm, clear morning sparkled in the valley and the church bells rang as clear as if they hung outside our window. We went into town. At Bazzotti's and Paolucci's everyone was outside sweeping and hoeing, and Rosanna was washing windows as if, instead of winter, it were the first warm day of spring. The town was in the streets. Liberated from the wind, people walked at their leisure, stopping, chatting, the shop doors open wide, the shopkeepers ranging up and down Il Corso farther than usual. Two of them were standing over a vase whose plant had been snapped by the wind, arguing. I told you it needed to be tied. I tied it. To a toothpick. To the wall. With a thread. What was needed was a good broom handle. Like the one up your *culo*. Two more shopkeepers drifted over and joined in. *Che peccato!* What a sin. It was the wind. It was him. Then a lady yelled down from a second story window, *"Assassini!"* Killers. They all burst into laughter.

By afternoon a different wind blew, slow, from the southwest, herding swollen black clouds across the sky.

"It's going to snow," Nonna said.

"How can you tell?" Candace asked. "Because the pigeons are cooing?"

"No," Nonna smiled. "Because it's cold and the clouds are black."

Heeding Nonna's forecast, we were wheelbarrowing wood down from the woodpile to just outside the kitchen door under the eaves when, as big as poplar-puffs in spring, snowflakes ghosted over the roof and little by little filled the valley. Low in the west, the sun peeked through slits in the clouds, lighting up the walls of Montepulciano with a last, wistful glow of golden light. Then it was gone behind the drifting curtains of snow. We were thrilled. We scraped the thin layer from the garden wall and had a snowball fight, wheelbarrowed down more wood, then went up the hill for a look at the house and the gardens turning white.

The *coppe* of the roof and wrought iron lamps protruding from the wall and the road whitened first, and the tops of the posts that shored the vines, and the beams of the naked arbor, and the forsaken handcart near the house. A flock of starlings swept overhead and hurried for refuge in the pond's toppled cane. Paolucci's pregnant cow gave a hearty bellow but it sounded muffled and far away in the drifting snow. We made more snowballs, it was easy now, and threw at targets near and far, at posts and trees, our chimneys and each other. It was getting dark. At an unfathomable distance behind the falling snow, the amber lights of town flickered faintly, like pulsars trembling in another world. We piled up a last load of wood, stopped in the *cantina* to get slices of *prosciutto* and a bottle of wine for dinner, and were heading for the house when a shadow rose above us on the garden steps. It was Paolucci wearing a big grin.

"*Che bello!*" I exclaimed, spreading my arms. How beautiful!

"*Porca miseria,*" he said. "*Mi sento come un bambino.*" Pig misery. I feel like a kid. Then said, "I couldn't stay inside." He helped me stack the wood under the eaves out of the falling snow, then we sat on the warped bench that was still dry beside the door, and watched the snow pack thick in the cypress, and on the *lentaggine* bushes. Candace came out with steaming cups of boiled wine and the fragrance of cinnamon filled the winter air. It was twilight. It snowed and snowed. We sipped the warm, bittersweet wine. "Rosanna is making *ciambelline* tonight," Paolucci said. "They'll be ready after dinner. Come and eat them while they're hot." I said we would, *assolutamente.*

"I love *ciambelline,*" Candace said. Paolucci emptied his mug, stood and buttoned his coat collar, said, "*A più tardi,*" until later, and vanished in the snowy dusk of the fast-approaching night.

"What on earth are *ciambelline*?" I asked Candace.

"I'm dying to find out," she said.

After dinner we bundled up. We put on down vests to keep out the cold, then ragged Irish waxed-coats to keep out the damp, scarves, mitts and hats, and we went. The falling snow hissed softly through the bushes and the night shimmered in the snow's strange light. The long leaves of *nespole* hung like sad donkey ears, and the garden steps were rounded by undulating dunes. We shuffled past the *corbezzola* and olives with sagging branches, and up the road, past the vineyard with its poles wearing tiny caps of snow. The road and ditches had dissolved into one. And still it snowed. We plowed deep furrows cutting across the fields and the faint glow from the Paoluccis' kitchen acted as our guide. When we opened the door, light poured into the night and snowflakes drifted like fluttering butterflies.

The Paoluccis were all at home, settled in the kitchen. The fire blazed, the gnarled stump of an olive shot tongues of flame through slits. Carla was on the small couch in the corner cutting out a skirt from paper patterns, Paolucci and Nonna sat on the little benches inside the fireplace—he was rebraiding a rope-belt for an olive-picking basket, and Nonna was knitting socks of raw wool. Rosanna and Eleonora were at the wood stove fishing sizzling rings out of a pot of hot oil. "*Ciambelline,*" Candace exclaimed. "I told you I loved *ciambelline.*"

"Donuts," I said.

"Wash your mouth out with soap," Candace said.

We sat at the big table covered by a crisp cloth, and Franco sent Eleonora to get a bottle of *vinsanto*, and Eleonora said she was busy why doesn't he get it himself, but she went anyway, and came back with the amber-colored wine. A great bowl of steaming, tantalizingly fragrant *ciambelline* were set in the middle of the table, then Rosanna brought a small pot from the stove, holding its hot handle in the corner of her apron, and she poured its slowly oozing golden contents over the *ciambelline*. "It's good with hot honey," she said. Nothing could have tasted better on a cold and snowy night.

"*Domani si fa festa*," Nonna said. Tomorrow's a holiday.

"Tomorrow, if the snow stops," Paolucci said, "we can walk down to the ruined mill and cut two Christmas trees."

"Maybe the snow will never stop," Eleonora said wistfully.

"In the old days it never stopped," Nonna said.

"It's true," Paolucci said. "One time it snowed for four days, and they had to cut a waist-deep trench in the middle of Il Corso for people to walk, but some were too lazy to cut a path to it from their door, and climbed down ladders from their windows."

"We couldn't drive out of here for a week," Rosanna said.

"*Che festa!*" Carla said. What a holiday!

We left late. The snow had slightly eased; we could just make out the gauzy lights of town. The snow on the ground was nearly to our calves and we stood in the road and watched glimmers of moonlight filter through the clouds.

"Let's go up to town," Candace said.

"You're crazy," I said.

"What's that got to do with the price of rice in China?"

I had no idea what that meant, and I was feeling too good to ask, so instead of turning homeward, we mushed up the road through the virgin snow.

The world seemed to be dressed for some great occasion: Paolucci's vines wore long, snowy necklaces; cypresses donned tall, white, pointed hats; the bare branches of elms were full of winter lace; and in Anselmi's yard the plows and carts had vanished and in their place were wondrous mounds and drifts of a new landscape.

The road steepened through a wood. The ancient cypresses of the cemetery loomed dark on their lee side, dark against the white night. When we climbed high enough, we looked back through the cypresses and over the cemetery wall. A white sea of waves rolled over the graves. But from under the snow, from each grave, glowed a hazy, rosy light. Through the narrow shafts that the eternal flames had rent, a diffuse light, like fleeing souls, shot toward the sky. A bell tolled above us. The snow kept falling.

"No wonder no one builds a house near a cemetery," Candace whispered.

We turned at the open shrine, stepped inside and sat on the narrow bench and rested. Below the hill, at the cemetery, the wind sighed and whispered in the boughs. We climbed on. Shrubs lay splayed and flattened by the snow, and the crotch of tree limbs cradled sleeping drifts. Through the great west gate we could see the town draped in winter white. A few lights twinkled above snow-packed windowsills, and gargoyles of snow perched on every chimney, every torch spike, every jut. Along the streets were undulating dunes of wind-carved, wind-smoothed snow.

Piazza Grande was softened by dunes and drifts and the wide, shallow stairs of the cathedral had vanished under a gentle slope. The light was still on in the little bar, and a man stood at the window gazing out. Another sat at a table looking nowhere. We went in. *Buonasera, buonasera.* We ordered and sat near the other window and drank steaming hot chocolates and then brandy.

"*Che silenzio,*" the man at the window said. What silence.

"Not like when we were young," the other smiled. "There was noise then."

"Lots of noise," the other said.

And they went on about some snowfall long ago, when the night was full of children yelling, laughing, tumbling in the snow; when Pietro sat on the flipped hood of a Cinquecento and had his dog drag him through town; and Beppe mushed about with wicker baskets for snowshoes; when the snowball fights in the Piazza never ended; when they all built a snow ramp to peek through the nuns' window; when Vittorio became *Il Missile Umano* by donning a fertilizer sack and launching himself head first from the church steps; and when someone's Mamma opened the shutters and yelled "There's school tomorrow," everyone stopped playing, turned, and filled her *soggiorno* with snowballs.

"*Che tempi,*" the barman said. What times.

Then the bar was closing and we bundled up and went out. *Buonanotte.*

The Piazza was silent and empty. A gust of wind was rearranging the drifts. The griffin and the lion on the stone well wore caps of snow, and still the snow swirled down. And, if we listened closely, we could hear from the empty arcade the fading echo of the snowball-fighters' voices, and see through the falling snow the explorer in his baskets mush ahead, and the dog tugging the hood of the Cinquecento, and on the church steps, through a veil of snow, the fearless *Missile Umano* launch again.

The bells tolled. It was midnight.

And it snowed and snowed.

EPILOGUE

*T*he snow lasted but two days, then the air warmed again and we returned to the garden. The winter days passed with long walks in the country, or trips to Florence or Rome, or drives to the sea to watch storms crash against the rocky coast. On cold but windless days, we would drive to the foothills of the old volcano to the tiny village of Bagno Vignoni, built not around a *piazza* but a great, steaming *vasca*, hewed from the limestone five hundred years ago and fed by hot springs. At a nearby rumbling waterfall that's almost too hot to bear, we swam in water milky with minerals, and stood under the hot cascade with steam billowing in the winter air.

We made visits to the small hill towns around us, and visits to our hill town to sit and chat in the cafes or read a paper, or on mild days to sit in the sun of Piazza Grande and watch our town live its life. We visited with friends, Bazzotti, Inaldo, Nebbia, and had meals with the Piccardis, and Gianni and Monica and of course the Paoluccis.

One by one we emptied the bottles of wine in our tiny *cantina*, and little by little we learned about Tuscany—its hills, its light, its art, its food and wine, and most importantly its simple, passionate, in-love-with-life people. And, almost in spite of ourselves, we learned to live and enjoy life as the Tuscans do—*piano, piano, con calma.*

Through the winter a pheasant kept us daily company. It wandered around the house, crowed its wine-voiced cry, pecked at the garden, at plants in the big vases, at corn and wheat we left for him under the leafless arbor. Then one warm morning we heard a cuckoo call below the olives in the hedge. A few days later, at sunset, from an abandoned drainage tunnel behind the house, a mamma fox came out and sniffed about, and after her tumbled and scrambled six tiny, fur-ball pups.

It was spring.